The Entrepreneur's Guide to Banks, Borrowing and the Practical World

Wisdom for

Recent Graduates

Dr. Barkat A. Charania

Bloomington, IN   authorHOUSE™   Milton Keynes, UK

AuthorHouse™
1663 Liberty Drive, Suite 200
Bloomington, IN 47403
www.authorhouse.com
Phone: 1-800-839-8640

AuthorHouse™ UK Ltd.
500 Avebury Boulevard
Central Milton Keynes, MK9 2BE
www.authorhouse.co.uk
Phone: 08001974150

This book is a work of non-fiction. Unless otherwise noted, the author and the publisher make no explicit guarantees as to the accuracy of the information contained in this book and in some cases, names of people and places have been altered to protect their privacy.

First published by AuthorHouse 11/18/2005
Revised Second Edition: 7/18/2006

ISBN: 1-4259-0660-5 (dj)
ISBN: 1-4208-1667-5 (sc)

Library of Congress Control Number: 2004099400

Printed in the United States of America
Bloomington, Indiana

This book is printed on acid-free paper.

DEDICATED TO

My parents, Samrat bai and Nimji bhai Charania,

who, even without a primary school education,

imparted to me worldly wisdom and spiritual insight,

To my late brother, Habib Charania,

who, though himself could not avail education beyond secondary school,

instilled in me the desire to pursue education, and who

educated me, mentored me, and made me who I am today,

And to my wife Perveen Charania,

who has extended me her unwavering support throughout last 35 years,

and has given me the gift of our three wonderful children,

Celina, Afshan and Imran.

Disclaimers

THIS BOOK IS MEANT TO CONTAIN ONLY THE BASIC INFORMATION FOR THE BUSINESS BEGINNERS ON MANY PERTINENT TOPICS. ENTREPRENEURIAL INDIVIDUALS CONTEMPLATING THE START OF A BUSINESS MUST SEEK THE ADVICE AND CONSULTATION OF LEGAL, FINANCIAL, AND TAX EXPERTS.

Gender Discrimination

Masculine or feminine gender distinctions used in the text in different places are merely arbitrary and not meant to be discriminatory. Male and female references are interchangeable in most instances

Table of Contents

Preface to First Printing

While at school or a university, students have many future plans. A major aspiration is to become an entrepreneur or a businessperson and be one's own boss. However, educational institutions are not focused on teaching practical, day-to-day knowledge. At the end of their education, or even sometimes in the middle (if they drop out), students suddenly find themselves facing the real and practical world. Although well-educated and fired up to attain their goals, they lack practical worldly knowledge. Today, the world requires everyone to be credit-savvy, insurance-informed, and a relationship expert. All this may be learned through developing a good network, acquiring general knowledge, and benefiting from the experience of others.

The content of this book is based on firsthand and personal experiences. I started selling toffees at the age of ten to earn an allowance. After my graduation in medicine, I pursued a post-graduate fellowship in surgery in the U.K., and a degree in law and history. However, being part of a business-oriented family, I was fortunate to have been involved in every aspect of business from an early age. Much of the advice that a reader can find in this book is based on my experiences in a broad variety of the business fields, everything from trading to manufacturing to service industries, including hospital administration, real estate management, and banking. While details of approaching any practical matter may differ from reader to reader, basic principles of how a situation should be approached generally hold true across the board. Young entrepreneurs will find a wealth of information in this book that I have acquired by experience and would like to share with readers.

In addition, this book may be particularly relevant as a primer for young school and college graduates who are new entrants into the real world and about to taste the experiences of a rough and tough practical world. It is important and prudent for the unwary to start understanding the practicalities of the world as quickly as possible to avoid any mistakes, which otherwise may haunt them later in life.

Today, banks are a part of our daily lives. In olden days, depositing the customer's excess liquidity for safety and convenience was the bank's main task. In modern times, banks have incorporated many other functions, such as consumer and commercial lending, credit-card processing, remittances, and insurance and investment services. However, the basic and the most important function of the bank is still a depository. They then use the deposits to advance the same as loans to borrowers.

One of the most common needs of an entrepreneur is to borrow funds to turn his dreams into reality. Lending being an important function of the banks coincides well with the entrepreneur's needs and, along with other services they provide, banks attempt to satisfy diverse needs of present-day business requirements.

We shall deliberate in this book mainly on the commercial-lending function of banks for business needs of entrepreneurs. These deliberations will also focus on creating and maintaining banking relationships. It will also include procuring conventional and Small Business Administration (SBA) guaranteed loans.

To maximize the benefits of banking relationships, the entrepreneurs ought to understand their responsibilities and obligations to banks. We shall try to evaluate this relationship from the banker's as well as from the customer's perspectives. Once the reason behind a bank's expectations is understood, your banking relationship will become friendly, pleasant, and mutually beneficial. It will then create better bonding between you and your banker. This will alleviate any reason for misunderstanding and acrimony between you and your banker. In short, this book is about being "street smart" while dealing with banks and bankers.

A successful business is the final product of many factors put together. Financing is an important element to start and run a business successfully. However, practical experience and knowledge of the business that one wants to pursue are two of the most important ingredients. When proper planning is added to these variables, the mixture is then a ripe recipe for success.

The book also includes some chapters that deal with general knowledge on a variety of subjects, like credit scoring, limited-liability entities, tax benefits that may be obtained by using them, and bankruptcy protection laws. These will be very useful to the entrepreneurs. Even many seasoned businesspersons will find the contents of some of these chapters interesting with many new concepts or redefined and clarified old concepts.

This book is intended to help every entrepreneur and fresh graduate to be a better-informed person, inquiring and asking the right questions when the time comes for one to hunt for a loan or enter a good banking relationship. It is also a commonly experienced fact that to get better service anywhere, one gains from having as much knowledge in advance as possible. This book endeavors to impart such knowledge to you about many practical issues.

For your convenience, I have added a summary of many chapters at the end for easier review of those chapters.

Best wishes to you, wherever you are in your personal development and goal achievement. Good luck and Godspeed.

Nov 2005

Preface to Revised Second Edition

I am grateful to my friends, colleagues and readers, who have very kindly pointed out a number of errors. They have also very kindly spent time to suggest some additions to make the book more useful. All the material has been revised, corrected, and updated. Special thanks to Malick Ismail and Abdul Lalani helping me do this.

I would welcome any further suggestions about adding some more material, to make this book more helpful to entrepreneurs and young graduates. Thank you all for your support.

Dr. Barkat Charania

June 2006

Email: Dr.Barkat.Charania@OilProducts.Biz

Acknowledgements

I would like to humbly convey my sincere thanks to all my friends and acquaintances who have directly or indirectly contributed to making this book a reality.

This book is a result of many personal experiences, extensive interviews, and discussions with relevant people and close friends like bankers, accountants, attorneys, entrepreneurs, and veteran business owners. All of them have been excited by the outcome of our various encounters in the shape of this book, and they have very willingly advised, commented, and critiqued the material being presented here. I am grateful to all of them.

I am thankful to my son Imran, daughter Afshi, niece Saleena Meghani, and colleague Shakil Kurlawala for showing me their dispassionate and objective day-to-day dealing in business. My daughter Celina has been a precious guide for bouncing off ideas on various aspects.

Young entrepreneurs continue to amaze and impress me with their agility, willingness to commit to hard work and learn quickly, their desire to embrace technology, and their superb education. Individuals that immediately come to mind are my nephews Adil and Rahil Jafry, Feisal Shariff, Nuruddin Abjani, and my children Imran and Afshi Charania. I admire their entrepreneurial initiatives. Their determination to succeed is striking.

I feel that some people have a gift of tackling any business issue with an angle of a resolving it. They understand and can explain the intricacies of business much easily because of their experience. I found such qualities in my nephews Anis Charania and Inayat Lakhani. They and Abdul Lalani, with many others from the business world, have been a continuous and invaluable source of advice while writing this book.

Many close friends, professionals with great wisdom, have been directly and indirectly a source of encouragement for me. The first one that comes to mind is Naeem Kohari, a finance wizard, who continuously supported the idea of writing this book. I would also like to thank many other experts in different fields whose advice has been invaluable. These are Musa Dakri, William Yeh, and Nasrullah Khan in the banking industry; Haroon Shaikh and Naushad Kermali in the accounting profession; and Anwar-e-Qadeer, Faisal Shah, and Celina Charania Shariff (my daughter) in the legal profession.

I am especially thankful to Shehzad Kurlawala for his extensive help in editing and proofreading.

Section One

Some Basic Facts

for All Entrepreneurs

Chapter 1

What Does It Take to Become a Successful Entrepreneur?

There are many ingredients to success in every field. Some of these factors are generic and are applicable to all circumstances, while others are specific to an individual situation. In business and entrepreneurship also, there are many generic and standard qualities and virtues needed from the entrepreneur. We shall try and define them here.

Ambition: This is by far the most important ingredient in becoming a successful entrepreneur. Without ambition to grow and be successful, many important and much-needed jobs will remain undone or less attended, leading to very slow progress or even failure. Hence, every beginner has to try and understand his own ambition and follow his or her sixth sense in starting or pursuing any career. Today's world is very competitive, and although ambition is an inborn thing, it would be safe to say that the competitive spirit, which is promoted in today's schools and colleges, sharpens the inborn ambition to a large extent.

Personal interest: You need to be interested from the bottom of your heart and spirit to be able to succeed in any line of work. One sure way to lose and fail is to start a job and lose interest in the middle. Hence, all entrepreneurs are well advised to have a long enough exposure in the line that they are wanting to pursue as career. Such exposure will make you understand how much interest you actually have in the career, which, on first look, seems to be enticing. You may have to work in that business or career for some time to understand its requirements. You then need to analyze from the experience obtained to understand the limitations and difficulties in that career and then conclude whether that business or career is suitable for you or not.

Commitment: To find success in any work, only getting involved is not enough. One has to be committed to the work. As an entrepreneur, you need to learn this early in life, so that you are trained to be absolutely devoted to the kind of work that you chose to pursue for your entire life. A new business venture is like raising a child. It is a challenge to learn many new things and be dedicated to do all that it takes. Again, if the commitment and interest is any less than the best, it may lead to mediocrity and/or failure. Many businesses do not do well only because the entrepreneur is not fully committed right from the beginning.

Experience: This is also one of the most important ingredients to bring success to any work. Experience is an invaluable asset that anyone can invest in one's work. We strongly advise every entrepreneur to work and gain experience in the line of work that you think will be interesting and gather a lot of experience before starting your own business. The time spent in obtaining such experience will reveal to you the limitations and rewards attached to it. It will expose you to many possible problematical situations and teach you how to resolve or rectify them. The firsthand experience will allow you to measure your own interest in that line of business and will also be a test if the interest is sustained after a while. Firsthand experience and an understanding of the business will also reveal whether or not this is the kind of work that you like. It will also be clear to you whether it will satisfy your future expectations and obligations to yourselves, your family, and community.

Planning: Well-experienced gurus will tell you that, generally speaking, "planning is best learned hands-on, while on the job." Good planning is based on the experience that you obtain from working in a business or from someone who already possesses such experience. Sound planning is a key to the success of any business. Any friends, financiers, or bankers who agree to support your enterprise will want to see that the planning of the venture is sound and well-thought-of.

Close supervision and management: This skill is a byproduct of the experience that you obtain and acquire while mustering experience in the field of work that you wish to pursue. Close supervision by the owner with appropriate experience is essential for any business to succeed. Statistically, one of the most important reasons for failure of any business is cited to be poor management. Therefore, the overall management of the business has to be vigilant. There are many aspects of the work in any business, and all those aspects need to be looked into regularly by the management to ensure the best performance. These include buying and selling the inventory, insuring the business adequately, hiring and firing of employees as needed, training, and interpersonal relationships, to name a few.

Investment: Apart from the investment of experience, which is abstract, the entrepreneur needs to have certain amount of tangible investment capital available to start any business. Surely the banks and financing institutions are there to assist the entrepreneurs, but no bank will extend all the funds needed for almost any business. All lenders would like to see a healthy debt-to-equity ratio before agreeing to loan that business. Not only is the investment the lifeline of any business, but also it has to be adequate and available when needed. Non-availability of finances and not arranging for it in good time is statistically the second most important cause of failure of a business. That's why, sufficient financing must be arranged well in time. Proper planning ensures that entrepreneurs avoid common mistakes, like securing a type of financing that may not fulfill the needs of that business, miscalculating the amount required as working capital, or underestimating the cost of borrowing money. We shall define these terms and explain them in detail, as they relate to what the lender might expect to see as an investment from the entrepreneur.

Luck: This may sound unscientific, but at the end of the day, luck plays at least some role in any and every work and situation. Business, be it any, is always a slight risk. By and large to a major extent, all the other ingredients are under the control of the entrepreneur. Nevertheless this luck factor is the sequel of unforeseen circumstances and situations beyond your own control. Nevertheless, this should not deter you, the entrepreneur to start a new business. Good wishes, along with support and prayers from the relatives, friends, and well-wishers, will surely boost the morals of the entrepreneur. The fact is that you must put in the utmost, optimum effort in the work that you have chosen as a career, or business, and leave it to destiny to have success in the venture.

Summary of Chapter 1

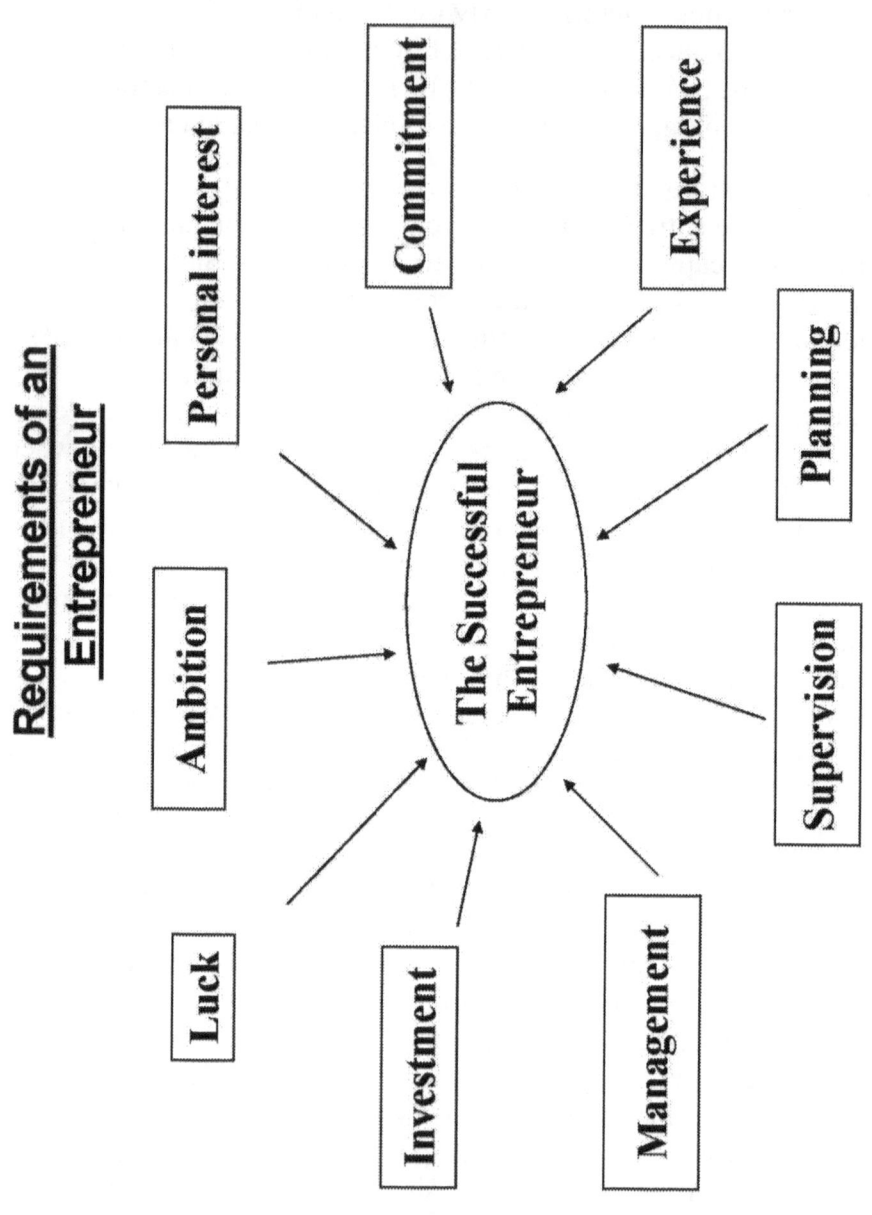

Chapter 2

Informal Sources of
Capital for Entrepreneurs

Entrepreneurs: If you are a person with an idea to start a new business or implement a new way of servicing a particular industry, you may be termed an entrepreneur. You may have thought of a new formula or a new invention and may have the right idea or vision to accomplish a particular goal. Now, to put your idea into practice, you need tangible capital, which you may not have. Hence, you would need to "raise funds" to try and make your dream come true.

You may have a long list of possible informal sources of raising funds to fulfill your dream and goal. However, when it is a question of parting with money, even the best of your friends and nearest of family will have many questions. The fear of losing the money makes the fund-raising a difficult task for the entrepreneur. Let us look at the list of all the possible sources of financing one by one to realize your dream idea.

Own money: You may have some valuable assets that you may liquidate, so that you can raise the capital that you need. It may be your car, home, jewelry, or other precious family treasures. However, this is not an easy decision. As mentioned earlier, any business carries certain risks, and one has to be convinced of one's likely success to be able to then risk all that one possesses into materializing one's dreams.

Borrow against your home or insurance policy: This is another easy way to obtain some capital. If this is enough, you may not need to look elsewhere. However, when this is not enough, or after employing such capital, you may have reached a stage where you need some more. That is the situation when you need some more funds to be raised through a loan, which we shall discuss in this book in detail.

Borrow on your own strength: In today's age, credit cards may come in handy, if your need is such that it can be satisfied by your limits on those cards. Although this may be an easy and quick fix to your need, you must understand that it may be very expensive, since the interest rates on credit-card debts are usually the highest. Consequently, you will need to replace this capital with a cheaper and more traditional source sometime soon.

Borrow from friends and family: This may also be one of the easier ways to finance one's goal of having a business, though it may not be the quickest. The entrepreneur will have to go great lengths to make the would-be financier understand that the money that he or she is about to part with will be used very carefully without much risk. The financier would also like to see that the money would be most likely returned in whole and with some reward. However, many times such personal arrangements may be interest-free or at a low interest rate, which can be beneficial while getting started.

Summary of Chapter 2

Informal Sources of Funds for Entrepreneurs

Borrow against Home Equity

Borrow against your Insurance Policy

Borrow against Credit Cards

Borrow from Friends and Family

Chapter 3

Formal Sources of Borrowing and Raising Capital

Financing your dream business: Raising necessary capital is one of the most basic activities in any business. Routinely this is achieved through borrowing in almost every business. Yet, it requires at least some preliminary understanding of certain concepts, without the experience of which, the process of borrowing may look and sound very complex to an entrepreneur. In a large deal, the borrowing process may even try out the acumen of an experienced businessman to its maximum. Asking for money is a difficult and daunting task in itself. On the other hand, if you do enough homework to prepare for this process, it will become relatively smooth and easy.

First, you will need to exhaust your personal sources of financing for your entrepreneurial needs, since that is perhaps the simplest and cheapest way to raise the finance that you are needing. However, if your needs are larger, or they cannot be served by the nontraditional ways of raising capital, as described in the previous chapter, you need to start doing some homework to apply for conventional or formal sources of capital. In this chapter we shall discuss the different formal sources of borrowing.

Age, size, and type of business: The process of financing differs for different situations, where borrowing is needed. The approach to financing and also its preparation will differ depending upon the size of capital that you need. You will also look at different sources depending upon the requirement and size of loan. If the requirement is for a small start-up business, usually the source to approach is different than if it is for a large or well-established business needing a large loan. A business that is a few years old and is already on its own feet may need additional capital to expand. While expanding, the business may require a larger cash flow, it may require new equipment, or the business may need to start an entirely new location to take over the competition. The sources of capital for such a need will be different from that of a start-up business.

9

For established businesses: An ongoing business, which is on its feet, growing and profitable, may also need capital to grow larger and acquire some upstream or downstream business lines connected with the original business. On the other hand, your business operations may have become larger, and its present shape and functioning does not allow you to capture all the potential profitability and opportunity. Therefore, you may need to expand its base with increased space, staff, and facilities. All these activities need additional capital. This is yet a different situation, where the capital providers may have specific strengths; for this reason, your choice of lending organization may be narrower and different.

Why borrow at all? At times you may wonder why borrowing is preferable over accepting an equity financing. There is a very simple mathematical explanation for this. Supposing you have two sources; one is ready to inject equity and another to raise a loan of same amount. Also suppose you wish to provide equal return to both sources, that is equity to be paid equal to the interest on loan. Now remember that the payment of dividend on equity is after the payment of tax. Hence, your business has to have made that much additional profit (equivalent to the tax paid on profits) to be able to provide an equity return (dividend) equal to the interest on loan. This may be large drag on the profits of the business.

Interest on borrowed money is an expense to the business and, hence, a tax write-off, which results in the business paying that much less tax. In other words, you can survive with lesser profit if you have borrowed from a lender than if you have accepted equity participation. This is why it is better to borrow, if your debt-to-equity ratio is healthy enough and is acceptable for the lender to provide a loan.

Aside from the above reason, when you accept equity in business, you are accepting a partner in the business, which may not always be beneficial because of many reasons. However, if you borrow instead, your only obligation is to repay the amount and not share your business and be accountable to any partner.

DEBT FINANCING

When looking for money, you must consider your company's debt-to-equity ratio. It is the relation between dollars you've borrowed and dollars you've invested in your business. The more capital the owners have invested in their business, the easier it is to attract financing. If your firm has a high ratio of equity to debt, you should probably seek debt financing (e.g., borrowing by way of a loan). This may take one of many forms depending upon what needs to be accomplished and what will suit both the borrower and the lending institution, like a bank.

Traditional sources: One of the most traditional and conventional ways to fulfill your financial need is through a lending institution, of which banks are at the forefront. Traditionally, banks have always been the primary source because not only do you get financing from them, but also you may use them on a daily basis for many of your transactional business needs. This book is mostly about such borrowing from traditional sources like banks or other similar lending institution. They will be discussed in detail in the following chapters.

Banks as traditional lenders: There are many formal sources of capital. Your decision to approach a particular lender will depend upon the business itself, its age, and its stage of progression. However, the most traditional of these sources, which comes to mind first, is the street bank. Banks may provide a conventional loan or an SBA-guaranteed loan, which will be explained in detail.

- **Lines of credit**: This is the most traditional form of getting the financing that is offered by most banks. This is the bread-and-butter business of almost all banks. These loans may also be tailor-made for the borrower as needed, when the bank is satisfied of a number of factors that they will be looking at about the eligibility for such a loan. Most important of these is the bank's confidence in the borrower that the bank's money will be paid back as per an agreement with an applicable and agreed interest rate. However, in reality and practice, this is a little more complex. The banks are regulated bodies and are audited by different agencies. Therefore aside from their own satisfaction, they need the borrower to conform to a number of additional conditions and obligatory reporting. Usually, these are simple requirements, like regularly providing financial reports, inventory levels, receivables, IRS returns, and any unforeseen changes that may have happened with the business, its owner, or in the industry itself.

- **Seasonal loan:** Utilization of these bank facilities depends upon the kind of business or industry you are in. For a seasonal business, a line of credit may be the best form of borrowing, since the business may repay as agreed, when the business is rich with cash at the conclusion of a season. The banks also need some "clean-up" or "cooling" period of up to four to eight weeks. This means that all of the borrowed amount must be paid in full for a certain period, as agreed, with zero outstanding balances. This is the bank's way of ensuring that the business does not start using the seasonal facility as an ongoing addition to their cash flow and that business is able to sequestrate and release that amount at least for a few weeks from their regular operation. Contrary to this, in the construction industry, you may need a cyclical increase of capital to compensate for some slow period in the industry, and the loan should be accordingly tailored through a discussion between the banker and the borrower.

- **Term loan:** A term loan is for a fixed period of time. The bank may want you to pay the interest and a portion of the principal over a fixed period of time, anything from two to five years. For regular businesses, this is a better way to use the money. In term loan the business owner will know in advance the outflow of cash every month in the form of repayment of principal with its additional expense of interest as cost of that capital. This allows you to correctly project the cash flow. The borrowed amount may be repaid as per an amortization schedule (fixed amount of money as monthly installments consisting of capital plus interest) over an agreed period of time.

EQUITY FINANCING

If your company has a high proportion of debt to equity, experts advise that you should increase your own capital injection (equity investment) by additional funds. That way you won't be over leveraged to the point of jeopardizing your company's survival. You may have to raise the equity from other sources. However, this means that you are offering a portion or share of your business to bring in a partner, someone who is ready to invest in your business.

This idea of offering a partnership of your business has many other consequences, which should be considered before finally deciding about it. Some of the most important of these issues are the control of business, the relationship of the partners, liability limitation for the partners who are not actively conducting business, and rewards in the shape of profit and appreciation for the investor in lieu of his investment. Such investor may be actively participating in business activities or may be a passive or silent partner. This is a subject in itself. Some of these may be considered as offering the securities and may need clearance from the Security and Exchange Commission (SEC). However, most of the small businesses may not need to undergo the strict scrutiny of SEC regulations. It is imperative, however, that if you start considering equity financing as an option, it needs to be understood by further reading and personal advice from professionals like lawyers and accountants.

Angel investors and venture-capital firms: There are individuals and firms who help expanding companies grow in exchange for equity or partial ownership. Most of these angel investors look for a potential company or business that is likely to return a relatively large profit if successful. As it happens in practical life, the larger the return, the bigger the risk. However, these venture capitalists are experienced in taking unusual risks.

OTHER CREATIVE SOURCES TO RAISE CAPITAL

The sources described below are not formal and common. These are some of the creative ways of raising capital usually for seasoned and experienced businessmen for a business that is already running.

Factoring account receivables: An experienced operator may find this to be a favorable method to raise the needed capital. Those businesses that have large receivables may find a company ready to provide cash against these receivables for a return. These factoring companies earn their profit by charging a fee for providing the upfront cash against receivables, which are going to mature for payment sometime in the near future, as per the terms of sale. By paying the upfront cash, these companies employ their own capital for the remaining period the debt needs to mature and, hence, take a small risk and provide the convenience of immediate cash flow. Their fee is to cover the time period for which they will tie up their capital and that certain small risk that they are taking.

Mergers and acquisitions: A profitable company, who still wants to grow further, may have some other avenues to look to. Another large company may be ready to merge it into a larger group or acquire this company and let it work independently. There are many reasons to go this route for both the companies. It reduces the competition for the larger company and provides a larger growth from the smaller company. In return, the smaller company gets the much-needed capital to grow as per their plan.

Purchase-order financing or vendor financing: Some of the companies are very good at managing their debts, which arises from their purchases of inventory, equipment, and other needs. With increasingly better relationships with the vendors, the buyer can gradually move their repayment period to longer periods of time and, hence, satisfy their short-term need of capital. With a good relationship, such funds are usually without interest.

Lease financing: This may be one of the ways to fulfill your need, particularly for equipment. It may be a little more expensive of a way, but the scrutiny requirements of a leasing company are usually less stringent and simpler. Its processing is also much quicker than a bank loan. Conceptually, the leasing company charges you rent on the equipment that they will buy and provide for your use, while also getting their investment back within some prescribed period. The rent will continue until the term of lease matures. If a lease-to-buy option is preferred, at the end of the lease period the ownership title will be transferred to the lessee at an agreed-upon very small price as per the terms of the lease.

Finance companies: Here is an overlap of the facility between banking and financing companies. Asset-based financing is usually the domain of finance companies, but most banks will also look at such a proposal. This is provided against the collateral of inventory and receivables in the shape of a revolving loan. However, there is one important difference between this and the revolving line of credit or term loan of a bank. In most cases of asset-based financing by the financing company, the lender would want the payment of the receivables to be made directly to them, which in turn is given again to the business in the shape of a revolving loan. Banks do not get involved in getting the payment from third parties, like your customers.

A finance company will ask for collateral in the shape of security interest in the inventory and receivables of the business. However, all lenders are in the business of "renting" out their money and not in the business of taking the possession of the inventory and trying to sell it if the loan goes sideways. In addition, the inventory is movable and is theoretically in possession of the borrower with a much smaller control by the lender, and, hence, a bigger risk as a collateral in the eyes of the lender.

Hence, receivables are always perceived as better collateral than inventory by some lenders. If the receivables have an acceptable aging history, they will mature as expected at a certain time, depending upon the industry practice and understanding between customer and business or services. For such a need, a bank may be a better source of financing, since they do not want the payment made to them by your customers, meaning there is no one between you and your customer. Therefore, a bank loan may be a preferable source of borrowing than a financing company, if the collateral of receivables and inventory are provided.

Mortgage Companies: Traditionally, the mortgage companies have been lending against landed property as collateral. This is the most common way of financing the residential properties. However, some mortgage companies, whose objectives agree with such proposals, also finance the commercial properties. This would be yet another source of capital for the business.

Summary of Chapter 3

Formal Sources of Funds for Entrepreneurs

Debt Financing

Banks and other Lending Institutions

- Line of Credit
- Term Loans
- Seasonal Loans
- Guaranty
- Letters of Credit

Equity Financing

Venture Capitalist
Angel Investors

Other Sources

- Factoring
- Mergers and acquisitions
- Vendor Financing

Chapter 4
Role of Banks in Today's Society

Concept of Bartering: In today's world, we need the banking facilities for various reasons. Back in olden days, all the transactions used to be on a barter basis. This was because most of the exchange of services or goods was local within a village or a town. A service could have been exchanged for any other service or goods from someone else. For instance, if you were a farmer, you would provide some wheat to a shoemaker to get a pair of shoes. Or if you were a doctor, you would provide your services in return for some clothes or eatables.

Concept of money: It is said that time is money. It is true. Within a given time frame, a person may do certain things to generate income and bring food for his family. If the work performed is more than his required immediate needs, the surplus will need to be stored. However, to be able to do that, such services or goods need to be evaluated and changed in the shape of money. This is called monetization of services or goods. It is such surplus work or commodities that brought in the concept of money.

Concept of quantification of services and goods: In the present, modern, industrialized world, the services and commodities are available in bulk. Many times the available commodity may not be needed by the would-be users when it is available and, conversely, the commodity may not be available when needed by the users. It is true for services also. Hence, the concept of "stocking up" the services and commodities started to take shape. As this developed further, gradually a concept of money was developed, which quantified the value of services and commodities. Hence, a quantity of services or commodities may be converted into money for its future use, since in practice, such services or commodities in their original shape may not be stored or retained for a long period of time.

Concept of globalization of exchange of services: The quantification and monetization of services and goods allowed a large quantity of services and commodities to be collected and stored in the shape of money for a future use. These varied services and goods could now be purchased or sold by their owners. This money, at that time, generally represented only the leftover portion of services, which was for use at some future time. However, as the businesses started becoming multi-focal, with branches in the cities, states, or even international, and with a concept of profit, the leftover surplus profits also needed to be kept aside safely in the shape of money. This process brought in, in a rudimentary form, the concept of asset building.

Concept of banks as third-party trustee of deposited money: With the passage of time people were required to put their excess "money" in some safe place. You may be surprised to learn that it was not very long ago, and even today in some countries of the world, many people think that the safest place to keep one's money is either in a mattress or in a hole dug in the backyard. But this is becoming rare and usage of banks as a depository place is all too common at least in the developed countries. The Glass-Steagall Act has remained one of the pillars of banking law since its passage in 1933 by erecting a wall between commercial banking and investment banking. Historically, the banks started doing all businesses related to money, and this included the transaction of securities, annuities, and the selling of insurance prior to 1933. (See Annex.) The Act stopped the banks from dealing with securities, in particular, and many other money-related activities to ensure a distinction between investment and commercial banking. However, this Act has recently been revised to allow the banks to indulge in other money- and business-related activities with certain limitations.

Conceptual role of alternative forms of money: As the economy has expanded, the use of physical money is becoming less every day and is being replaced by "plastics," or credit and debit cards. Even these cards are being less frequently used physically as the Internet and e-commerce take over, in which all you need to give is a number representing your checking or credit-card account, from where the money may be withdrawn.

Presently, banks have a large role to play in our day-to-day activities. A vast majority of us are workers in one or more jobs. Our salaries are directly or indirectly deposited into our designated bank accounts. A majority of our recurrent monthly obligations are paid from this pool of money held by our bank. Such activities that immediately come to mind are utility bills, mortgage payments, credit-card bills, buying against check writings, and payment of supply invoices for individuals. Businesses also use the bank services similarly, plus they pay the invoices of their inventory buying, supplies, insurance, day-to-day business expenses, and so forth from their bank accounts by writing checks.

Concept of banks assisting you in your accounting and bookkeeping: The economy is expanding in most of the industrialized world. The WTO (World Trade Organization) and its predecessor GATT (General Agreement on Tariffs and Trade) have obligated everyone with the imposition of their strict code of rules for all kinds of businesses to document the transactions to almost their full extent. However, the requirement of full documentation has indirectly benefited the businesses and individual users by its inherent advantages of creating a supplementary or sometime even primary instrument of bookkeeping.

Concept of banks as your referee: Aside from all the above, in today's world we require references to do our business. There will be many professionals that you will need to involve in your business like attorney, CPA, brokers and your banker. Amongst these, whenever a reference is needed, your banker's recommendation will be considered very respectable. Everyone is almost obligated to create such networking with other professional business associates to ensure its positive influence on your ability to create further opportunities. Such relationships and references then help you to increase revenues of your business and, hence, bring in larger profits.

Summary of Chapter 4

Evolution of Banking

Bartering of goods and services

Surplus goods and services deposited in the shape of money

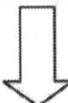

Usage of those deposits for Lending To borrowers in need

Chapter 5
Banking Is a Mutual Relationship

Bank accounts: Today it will be rare to find someone in the U.S. managing without a bank account or banking relationship. It has become a need of the day to have a bank account and banking relationship, because many of our day-to-day money transactions have become bank-dependent. These include many installment and utility payments like electricity, telephone, gas, auto, home mortgage, insurance, subscriptions and others.

Consumer banking: Even on the consumer side, with the advent of credit cards, debit cards, and availability of checking and savings accounts, numbers of cash payments are reducing drastically, while the overall number of transactions may be the same. We find many people pulling out checkbooks or a plastic card for even small grocery buying or for a meal in the restaurant. This practice provides an additional advantage of keeping accurate records of all expenses. Many companies nowadays like to deposit your salaries and wages directly into your bank accounts. Hence, if you mostly pay your bills with credit cards, debit cards, or checks, you do not get to see all that many dollar bills, and you do not need to carry a lot of cash, which may be risky in many situations.

Business relationships with banks: In retail banking the banks have been very aggressive in consumer loans. These include car, home, appliances, home equipment, and gadgets. However, when we talk about banking relationships, we mean borrowing from banks for business needs. It is this aspect of relationships with banks that requires you to be formal, businesslike, and disciplined. In business, both you and the lender would wish such relationships to grow and be long-term, mutually beneficial, and trustworthy, as your needs increase.

Importance of the relationship: There are two specific, imperative functions of the bank as perceived by the new businessman or an entrepreneur. One is the provision of the capital for the business when needed, which if the business is a success and remains ongoing, keeps on increasing. Second is the intangible value of a relationship with banks as a referee, consultant, and advisor when needed.

A good relationship with your bank also provides an entrepreneur with a stepping stone to climb over many hurdles in the way of being a successful businessman. Once started and on its way with a good note, it is almost a lifelong investment in a public-relations exercise. With success, the entrepreneur also needs the right kind of references to grow to the next higher step with the help, assistance, and good will of his banker.

Growth of the relationship: Since this relationship is very important for the entrepreneur to cultivate and nurture to grow nicely, this book provides some practical tips to help that happen. Explanations in these pages allow you to put yourself in your banker's shoes, so that you know their angle of thinking and where they are coming from. If you understand why they want so many reports from borrowers on regular basis, you as a borrower will be more responsive, and your dealings with your banks will become very congenial and fruitful. A borrower must understand that there are laws to strictly regulate the banks. Hence, they also have a job to do to keep their auditors and regulators happy by keeping your loan file as complete as possible, so that no auditor or regulator raises any objections or concerns. Once this is understood, the rest of the borrower and banker's relationship is just a simple public-relations exercise.

Regulators for the banks: Business lending by banks includes many types and many reasons. Banks are in the business of seeking deposits from the depositors and allowing businesses to use them in the form of loans. While doing so, though, the banks have a fiduciary responsibility to act as trustee for the depositors. To make sure that the banks do fulfill this responsibility, the government has created several agencies to keep a close eye on banking activities. This is in the shape of audits by regulators from state and federal agencies, such as the FDIC (Federal Deposit Insurance Corporation) or OCC (Office of Controller of Currencies). All these agencies are charged with responsibilities to ensure the banks do their business in a prescribed manner. The most important factor that the regulators like to probe is that the banks are not taking any undue risks, jeopardizing the depositor's dollars in the process.

Federal Deposit Insurance Corporation (FDIC): FDIC was created in 1933 after the Great Depression. Its job is to protect the depositors against losses if the banks fail for any reason and go bankrupt. This has happened again recently in the eighties and, hence, the role of the FDIC has become important. There are other federal agencies that also supervise banks to ensure that their operations are according to the prescribed laws. The FDIC is a federal insurance scheme that the banks buy to protect their depositors. This simply means that all the depositors in such an FDIC-insured bank have an insurance up to $100,000 for each of their accounts in case the bank gets into financial problems and fails. Therefore, the FDIC being the insurance underwriters would like to ensure that they are not unduly exposed. This is the reason for their periodic yet regular audits of the insured banks. The FDIC will get the banks to take necessary steps to protect the deposits of the public by getting them to stick to FDIC's prescribed instructions of safety while conducting the banking operations.

Your obligations arise from regulators' needs: A bank's workings are many times the reflection of the needs prescribed by these agencies. This may be frustrating to an entrepreneur since he or she is new and does not know the exact rules of the game. Sometimes they think that the banks are trying to unnecessarily harass them by pressurizing them to submit a lot of reports and paperwork, the objective of which they do not quite understand. These demands by banks at the behest of the requirements of the regulators may be almost exasperating to a businessman, but are required to be fulfilled eventually in the best interests of all concerned.

Start thinking as a banker to be a good borrower: We have always maintained that the best way to anticipate anyone's reaction is by putting yourself in their shoes. The relationship between entrepreneurs and their bankers is one good example. You need to develop this relationship in a positive way to ensure that your bank always remains your friend instead of your adversary when you most need them. No school or university teaches this particular aspect of life and business about how a good ongoing relationship between the bank and the customer is fostered, although it is very essential to avoid any unnecessary pitfalls. This learning comes by experience only, and sometimes, unfortunately, by the time the entrepreneur or a new businessman learns about it, it may perhaps be too late.

Banking is a regulated business: Operationally, banking is a business, and like any other business, it has its own capital and deposits of the depositors to lend to borrowers. Banks need to make money to stay in business. Banks also need customers to lend its money to, so that it makes money.

Obligations of a bank customer: In the banking business, there are certain obligations that the customers need to fulfill. If the customers are not fully aware of these obligations at the outset, they are likely to play foul in the eyes of the bank and its regulators. This ignorance, unawareness, or misunderstanding is one of the main reasons for the problems between the bank and its customer. In this book I have translated my and my colleagues', whom I have acknowledged in the preface, lifelong experiences with banks and bankers to try to provide and arm young entrepreneurs with a tool, or call it a weapon, to get the best out of their banking relationship. The life-size experiences from our learning will provide a template or a platform to do that. These pages will provide the new business owners an understanding, as to how to always be on the right side of this relationship. This will also prevent any unpleasant incidences arising out of a lesser understanding of the responsibilities that the customers must undertake while developing a relationship with their banks.

The borrower or the businessman must understand that the banks have to make you fulfill all those requirements, and then present them to the regulators to show them that they are working according to the guidelines of such regulating agencies. If they do not do so, their loans may be "criticized" or "observed upon." If this happens, there may be a lot of negative repercussions for all concerned. Such criticism or observation is often taken to be a black dot on the workings of the bank officials and bank itself.

Understanding the obligations: It is not only useful but imperative for the borrower to understand the reason for such onerous-looking requirements by their banks as part of the terms and conditions while lending the money and keeping the loan file in a good order. Once this is understood well, the relationship between the bank and customer will be very smooth. And this is the very purpose of this book. We sincerely hope and wish that all bank customers understand the angle from which their banker is coming from, by reading this book, and such other material, and thereby have a better and meaningful association with their bankers. This will make us feel that we have achieved our goal.

Facility creates mutual obligations: As you would have realized by now, for the most part, this book is concerned about getting the best facility from your bank or lending institution and then how best to maintain it through a smooth relationship. When such facility is created, there are certain considerations and obligations on the part of both parties to this relationship. This is what is mostly explained with the background of personal experiences and the advice of some seasoned bankers. On the face of it, this relationship seems to be lopsided in favor of the banks, meaning that in most circumstances it seems that it is the businessmen or the entrepreneurs who need the bank and not vice versa. This is not at all true. Banks cannot do without you. Please understand that the banks and lending institutions are also businesses. Banks and other financial institutions also need the customers like YOU, as much as you need customers for your own businesses.

Over a period of time, it has become an accepted way of practice that usually the clients approach the bank and not the other way around. However, you will be surprised how often, sometimes in subtle ways and sometimes very overtly, the banks are soliciting customers. The main difference between a bank's business and yours is that you employ your own capital and oblige your other resources and yourself in your businesses. The bank's own capital is usually a small percentage of its total loan portfolio. The bank uses public's deposits to satisfy their loan demands. This, at times, makes the depositors highly vulnerable to the bank's bad lending decisions. This is why two groups of people called auditors and regulators appointed by the government continuously look over the banker's shoulders to ensure that they are doing everything as required of them by the law and regulations and that they do not put others' deposits at risk.

Stay on the right side of your lender: It is this function and relationship building that we have concerned ourselves with in detail here in this book. As mentioned elsewhere, banks have their own requirements to stay on the right side of the regulators and auditors. While trying to avail these facilities, sometimes business owners do not remain cognizant of the bank's needs. It is not because they do not want to comply with the requirements, but it is because they sometimes think of them as trivial and futile. This misunderstanding sometimes finds the business owners on the wrong side of the bankers, causing an unnecessary friction. To achieve maximum benefit from their banking relationship, they should comprehend the banker's perspective of the whole scenario.

Relationship loan: A large proportion of small businesses will need the banking relationship for the kind of facility called "relationship loan." It is named such so as to show the importance to the value that your close relationship with the banker creates for you. On many occasions, when the loan department looks at your financials and analyzes them, the results may not be quite satisfactory to underwrite that loan. However, your banker knows you better than how the papers show your business profile. And, consequently, he may be comfortable in extending the loan you are asking for, although the supporting papers may not strictly justify the approval of the facility.

Section Two

Borrowing: an Intimidating

Task Made Easy

Chapter 6

Steps in Applying for Bank Facility

Borrowing is an intimidating task, and the procedure involved may at times be exasperating. However, we shall try and summarize our discussion about borrowing by detailing every step in the application of borrowing. This will allow us to understand each of the stages in borrowing discipline, and, hence, remove any confusion and undue worry. We shall then explain each of these stages in detail in the following relevant chapters.

Identification of your need: The first step is to identify the capital that you need as a loan, or any other facility that you need from the bank. This will depend upon the stage of progress in the business that you are in. You may be starting a business, in which case your need will be different than an established business.

Identification of your lender: This is the next step that you need to define. Some lenders specialize in one industry, while others are not quite comfortable to lend in that one. For example, some banks specialize in foreign business and letters of credit, others may do only the consumer loans, while yet other banks may do term loans, and SBA loans. Finding a right lending institution will require some due diligence, advice, and information seeking from experienced people around you. They should be able to give you some direction as to which lender or bank to approach. Your professional colleagues, like CPA and attorneys, would be very helpful in directing you to a right source.

Meeting with your lender: If you have identified the lender as your local banker, it is very easy. With the right introduction, you may set up a time to meet him/her and explain your plans and needs.

Loan application: This is an involving process. This will entail collecting a lot of information about yourself and your business. It is not only the information you know about your business, but some may be information that you may not even be aware of that the lender will want to know, like your competition and overall

31

industry that you are going to be in. Sometimes the information required for you to support the loan application may be so much that it may turn into an educational process for the borrower. However, the more information you provide, the better it is for the banker to decide about your application quickly, the more you learn about your industry, and the better it is for your business.

Loan application packaging: There are certain people and agencies who specialize in assisting you in compiling the loan application for presentation to your lender. They charge a small fee to do this work. If you are a novice, it will be a great help, since they know to a large extent as to what is required by the lender in the loan application.

Commitment letter: This is a letter from a lender to the borrower tentatively agreeing to provide the loan that he requires. There are certain terms and conditions that are spelled out. Some of these conditions define what their charges will be in terms of interest if they provided such a loan, while others are conditions that need to be fulfilled to make this commitment turn into a reality. This may contain that they expect the appraisal of the property, which is being provided as collateral, to appraise at a certain value. It will also provide for the condition that the property in question will be environmentally sound and comply with laws.

Processing of the loan application: Once the commitment letter is issued and accepted by the prospective borrower, the lender starts to process the loan. This is also called underwriting. The people in underwriting department of the lending institution will try and ensure that all the information provided in the application is verified. They will look at the figures provided in the loan application to match with their guidelines of acceptance of the risk of providing such loan. They will dot all the i's and cross all the t's before approving a loan.

Approval of loan: Once the loan is approved, the borrower may still have to provide some information that the lender may have requested. The next stage will be what they call the funding of the loan. This is done at the closing of the loan.

Closing: This is done usually at the lender's office or at a title company, who represents both the interests of the lender and the borrower. They charge certain fees to ensure that all the documents are in place at the time of closing. They also will ensure that proper liens are filed and the funds are made available to the parties at the discretion of the borrower.

Summary of Chapter 6

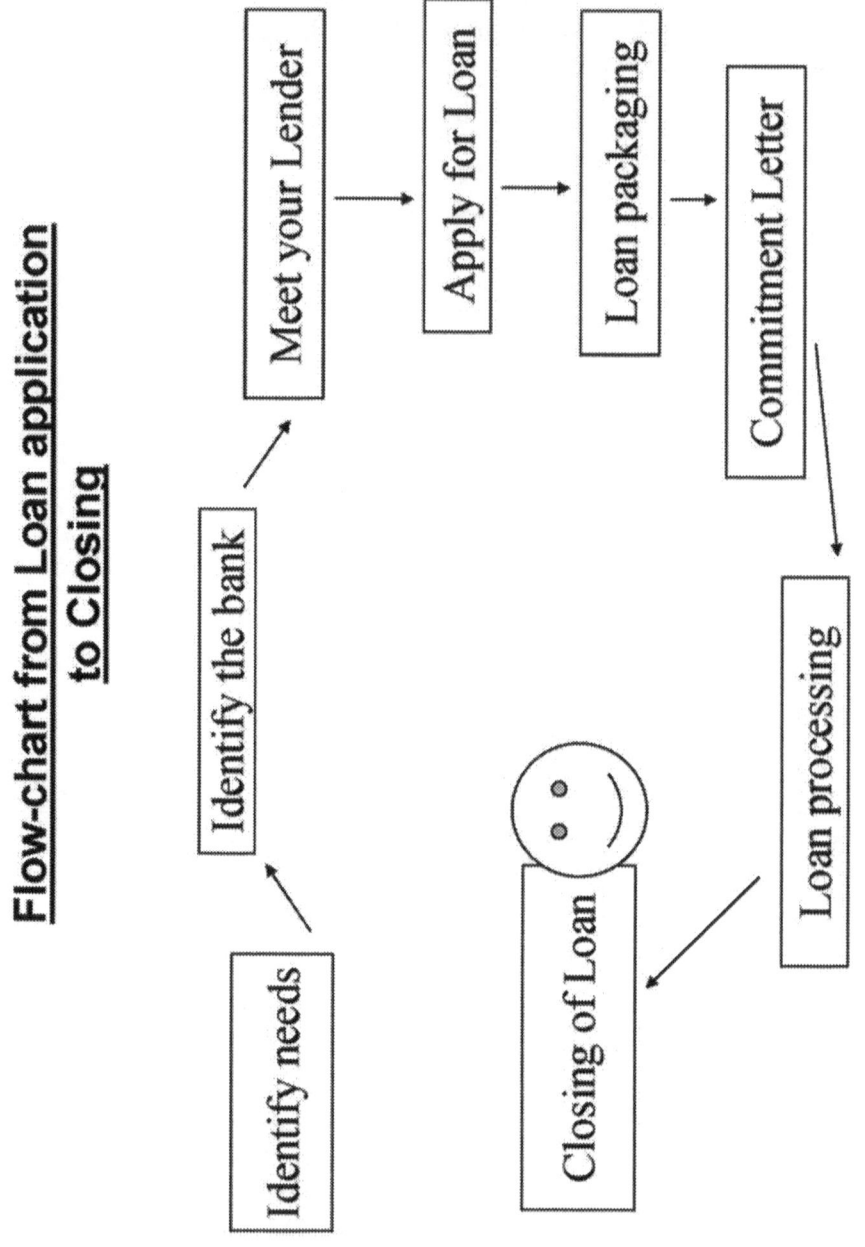

Chapter 7

What Types of Banking Facilities Are Available?

There are many functions of a bank, which are all offered as facilities to its customers. Although in this book we shall concern ourselves mostly with borrowings, we shall also describe other important functions of banks in short to familiarize the reader of other facilities available if needed. With regards to the loan, every loan is different from the other. All business owners and their CEOs need to identify their own needs, so that the facility can be almost tailor-made for their purpose.

Day-to-day banking: We all use many banking facilities almost every day. Generally, these banking activities mostly pertain to our depositing enough funds from our salaries or other incomes into our accounts and then disbursing those funds for different uses as needed. The deposits may be daily, weekly, or monthly, depending upon the revenue, or salary, income stream. Some of the disbursements need to be weekly, like salaries and wages or pocket expenses; others are monthly, like the utility bills, mortgages and others. Similarly, yet other disbursements, like property tax and related expenses like insurance, may be annual.

Depository function of banks: Aside from these daily activities of consumer banking, one of the most important functions that the banks do is keeping deposits, arising from the savings of their clients. Banks provide relatively safer environment for such deposits. Such environments are created by the society through the laws, rules, and regulations that the banks have to comply with. This, in turn, gives the depositors a sense of safety and satisfaction that the banks are using their deposits in an appropriate manner.

Lending function of banks: While working as a trustee for the depositor's money, the banks also found themselves being asked to lend money by many of their clients. Some of the customers who are in business may need additional funds in their businesses to be utilized in any of the many varied area, like developing their businesses, meeting their cash-flow needs, acquiring machinery or equipment useful to the operation of the business, or expanding the business as a whole.

Consequently, the banks found themselves as an intermediary for the safekeeping of their depositors' money and using the same money at their good discretion to lend to someone who needed it and was ready to pay it back with interest on that money. This is what has been alluded to as the business of the bank. They pay a suitable interest to the depositors and charge a similarly suitable interest (or "rent" for the usage of money, as has been referred to simplistically) to their borrower. It is this business of the banks that may be termed as buying and selling the "use" of the money that we are going to be mainly interested in this book. When a borrower needs a loan, the need of the bank to find a safe "home' for their depositor's money creates that lender-borrower relationship, which is central topic of this book.

Business function of banks: Putting all this in a simpler way would be something like this: Surplus money arises out of profits or savings and are kept at the bank by one customer, on which the bank pays some interest. The same money is then reinvested to satisfy the needs of another customer, who is a borrower and who pays a usage fee for that funding plus the overheads of the bank, so that bank may maintain all this activity and still make profit itself. Hence, in actual practice, the main business of the banks is buying and selling usage of the money, and while doing so, keep a profit for themselves.

We may take a simple everyday example. When a depositor opens a cash deposit (CD), he may be given, say, 3% interest if he keeps it with bank for a year. The bank, in turn, lends the same money to a borrower, say, at 7%. There seems to be a spread of 4%, which looks large. But then, the bank is a business and has its overheads. A major portion of this goes into paying the overheads and a small portion goes into their profit, which they are entitled to, while taking a risk of their own capital if the loan goes bad.

Regulators' interest in a bank's workings: Since the depositors of the banks are members of the public, the government would like to ensure that their money is safely kept, and prudently and equitably used. Regulators have some strong laws in place to support the economy by the supply of money from the public's savings. This is not just a cursory interest on the part of the government, since proper management of demand and supply of money will promote the economy and create jobs. Conversely, if this function is not supervised closely, there may be deleterious influence on the overall economy of the country. If the government does not create a machinery to supervise this function the liquidity may be channeled into non-development projects, or the banks may indulge in irresponsible and weak loans, causing pilferages or even embezzlement.

Hence, the regulators have specific laws enforced by a regular check on the health and working of the banks in the shape of auditor visits, along with state and federal regulators ensuring that everything that the banks do is strictly within the guidelines of the regulations and laws. If a borrower understands the obligation of the banker to these regulating agencies, which is for the good of the public at large, he will almost never be foul to such needs. Because of regulator's requirements the banker may ask for some seemingly unnecessary paperwork and supporting documents. Yet, complying to such needs and requirements of the lender, how-so-ever trivial you may think it is, is the key to a very smooth and beneficial long-term relationship of an entrepreneur with his bank.

Now let us see what facilities the banks provide, particularly in this narrow view of "lending" the money. Although we shall be mostly concerned with cash lending, it will be easier to understand some of the concepts where noncash lending is also provided by the bank as an institution.

Noncash facility by banks: On many occasions, entrepreneurs and new businesses will need some noncash facility instruments. These instruments create a contingent liability for the banks and, hence, they treat them with equal prudence as they do with cash lending. These facilities will be like providing guarantees,

letters of credit, or

bridge financing on uncollected funds or

conceptual overdrafts.

Although these are noncash facilities, the user client must not underestimate their value. If the customer does not fulfill his obligations by doing what he has promised when needed, the banks are then fully exposed to make equivalent cash available to the party to whom such a promise has been made. The bank will then look upon the client to quickly reimburse the amount as agreed without the slightest delay, since this will be termed as a default of the customer. However, since a large percentage of businesses in the U.S. do not require guarantees or letters of credits on a regular basis, we shall only briefly touch upon these activities here.

Guaranty: The banks provide guaranties to its creditworthy customers upon application. In a simple example, the guaranty may be in the form of an assurance to a landlord for a predetermined payment of rent for occupation of a space if unpaid by the lessee. The landlord may agree to accept the assurance in the form of a guaranty from the lessee's bank instead of cash deposit. The bank, as an intermediary, agrees to pay if the rent is not paid by the lessee when due. This is good enough for the landlord, since he gets this assurance from a recognized bank, which will fulfill the obligation if lessee does not. And then it remains between the lessee, who is a customer of the bank, and the banker to sort it out in case of a default, since the landlord has been paid by the guarantor bank.

The landlord does not have to even worry about the creditworthiness of the lessee, since that risk has been taken over by his bank. As indicated earlier, although this is a noncash transaction, it is a contingent liability for the bank, and it has to be recorded thus in their book for the regulators to see. For all practical purposes, the bank will need all the documents that it would otherwise need to create a loan of an equivalent amount, since if it has to be paid in cash in case of default by the customer, it will become a loan to the customer on whose behalf the guaranty has been issued.

In actual practice in the business world, the guaranty has a much larger role and is taken very seriously, since in businesses large amounts of money are involved that needs to be guaranteed.

Letter of Credit (LC): These are negotiable monetary instruments used between two business parties, with a bank in between. The most important feature of this instrument is that it is irrevocable, which means that once it is established and sent to the beneficiary's bank, it cannot be cancelled. This may be local, national, or international in scope. The purpose of such an instrument in simple words is that the seller is provided with a comfort that he will be paid for his goods by the buyer, since the buyer has to establish such Letter of Credit with a recognized and acceptable banking institution in favor of the seller or the beneficiary. The bank then pays to the seller when certain agreed conditions are met by him.

GATT (General Agreement on Trade and Tariff) has agreed on a Uniform Letter of Credit format, which is now used by almost all the interested parties. This is most useful in the international businesses between two parties in different countries. In such a situation, the business may be transacted via phone and fax correspondence, and the customer and vendors may not have even met each other. However, both parties require the surety of reaching their respective goal. Buyer would want to get the goods in return for payments and seller would want payment for his goods. This comfort is provided by the banks as an intermediary with an instrument like Letter of Credit.

This is a noncash facility by the bank to its customer, when the LC is established. Depending upon the relationship between the bank and its customer, the LC may be established by the bank at an agreed discounted deposit, instead of having to pay the full amount of purchase some time in advance. This is particularly useful when the trade is international and may take several weeks or even months from the order to the receipt of goods by the buyer. This spares the buyer from having to put up the full amount of money at the time of ordering. Conversely, it gives the seller a sense of certainty of payment, depending upon the type of LC established by the buyer.

There are several types of standard LCs, and many terms and conditions may be included. These conditions have got to be met by the beneficiary to get the payment. This payment may be instant (in "sight" LC) or in deferred terms (in "DA" type LCs), which is agreed upon by both parties before placing an order and establishing the LC by the opener. Those businesses using such facility would need to learn more about it from their bankers.

Timing of the loan application: It is important for any business to stay liquid enough to fulfill its payment obligations on a day-to-day basis. Hence, a close watch on cash flow will tell the manager or owner when he would need the loan facility. This has to be arranged in advance, since it may take a few days or even weeks for the bank to agree to your request to provide such a loan. Such a close eye on the liquid aspect of the business will help the understanding of how, when, and the extent of banking facility is needed in the shape of a loan that needs to be applied for and created in good time. That will help avoid any heartburn and worries or sleepless nights over imminent issues that may arise the next morning if some bills are not paid, checks are not honored, or some closing deadlines are lapsing. Such facility, if arranged in time may not allow losing some good opportunities also, if the financing is available.

Bridge financing of the uncollected funds: In normal business practice there is continuous incoming and outgoing cash from the accounts. This means there is a continuous stream of checks coming in and being deposited in your bank account. Simultaneously, your business has to keep on writing checks to your service and inventory provider.

It is the nature of business that although your incoming and outgoing cash generally match, it does not necessarily do so absolutely regularly on daily basis. This means that sometimes you have surplus funds in your account, whereas at other times your account does not have enough balance to satisfy the outflow caused by the amount of checks that you have issued to your vendors. This means your banker has to decide whether or not to pay your checks when presented. For you, it is a matter of reputation if the checks are not honored by your bank. It might affect your future ability to do the business with the same vendors, who might look upon you as a doubtful paymaster.

This situation has two aspects that need to be looked upon and discussed. One, which is mentioned earlier, is that you may not have the balance to satisfy the check presented for payment. And the other is that you may have deposited a check from your customer, which still has to go for collection through a correspondent bank or clearinghouse of checks.

Temporary overdraft facility: Such a situation necessitates that you have an arrangement with your banker to allow you bridge financing. This financing facility may have to be an overdraft, which means the bank allows you to draw or pay on your behalf at your request through your check that is over and above the balance that you may have in your account. However, it is always better to arrange with your banker to allow you bridge financing on your uncollected funds. The latter is easier for the bank, since they have a check from your customer in their hand that has to go through a routine clearing and, when cleared, your account will be positive again. The former is more difficult for the bank to agree to, since that will mean allowing you a signature overdraft without any collateral. However, in both situations you need to have an arrangement with the bank beforehand to meet such contingencies, so as not to spring any surprise on your banker and also not to face a situation whereby your bank has dishonored one of your important vendor's check, causing you to explain to them as to what happened.

Apart from the above-mentioned facilities, there are hoards of assistance that new businessmen and old ones alike may find beneficial from their banks. This includes advice, guidance, and support in many different ways from the bank and banking relationship that entrepreneurs may get. Bankers are very profuse in advising about businesses—of course, without taking any liability. They have a lot of experience in many businesses, since they have seen feasibilities on many varied businesses. They also know how it works in a very intricate way. It is because they have been involved in the inside track of the businesses while trying to ensure that the investment that they have made in it remains safe and secured.

Comfort level of the lender: For any loan to happen there has to be enough comfort level for the banker. One word of caution: the bankers are generally more conservative than the entrepreneurs— so much so that they may be skeptical or even cynical of some businesses. Sometimes an entrepreneur may be very confident of a business and its feasibility; however, when the proposal is seen by the lender, he may think otherwise. This may be because the lender may have seen such businesses not quite making the light of the day. While that's happening, the owner may lose his money while taking the bank's money with it. And the banks are trustees of the depositor's money, which is their fiduciary responsibility, and they must take it very seriously.

Bank loans of different kinds: It is a general misconception that small businesses do not get enough support from banks when they need to borrow money. It is because, as has been mentioned elsewhere, BANKS MAKE MONEY BY LENDING MONEY. However, the inexperience of many small business owners in financial matters often prompts banks to deny loan requests. Requesting a loan when you are not properly prepared suggests to your lender that you are a high risk. The banker's fiduciary responsibility to his depositor, whose money he is likely to lend to the borrower, will stop him from making any such loan, which might jeopardize the interest of the depositor. To ensure that the banker has the depositor's interest foremost in his mind, the FDIC auditors and regulators in general keep a hawkish eye on the business of the bank itself.

This whole exercise sometimes seems to defy the very purpose of financing. That is, when the borrower is weak, the bank may not be very keen to lend; whereas when the borrower is strong, and when the bank feels confident of their borrower, the borrower may have many sources that he can tap from. However, this is a simplistic overview of the whole subject. As described earlier, the bankers being the trustees of the depositor's money have to ensure that they are lending to a right entity or business, from where the repayment is almost guaranteed. This all results in a balancing act on the part of the bank and the borrowers.

To successfully obtain a loan, you must be reasonably experienced, prepared, and organized. You must know exactly how much money you need, why you need it, and how you will pay it back. You must be able to convince your lender that you are a good credit risk.

Terms of loans: These vary from lender to lender, but there are two basic types: short-term and long-term.

Short-term loans: These have a maturity of up to one year. These include working-capital loans, accounts-receivable loans, and lines of credit.

Long-term loans: These have maturities greater than one year; typically, these may be anything between five to fifteen years. Real estate and equipment loans may have maturities of up to twenty-five years. Long-term loans are used by major businesses for expenses and outlays such as purchasing real estate, facilities, construction, durable equipment, furniture and fixtures, vehicles and others.

Other facilities and loans: The businesses are almost always in need of more funds. These may be for:

working-capital and cash-flow needs,

buying new equipment,

merging into another business to make the existing business more profitable and viable, or

acquisition of new businesses by an existing business or by an entrepreneur.

Summary of Chapter 7

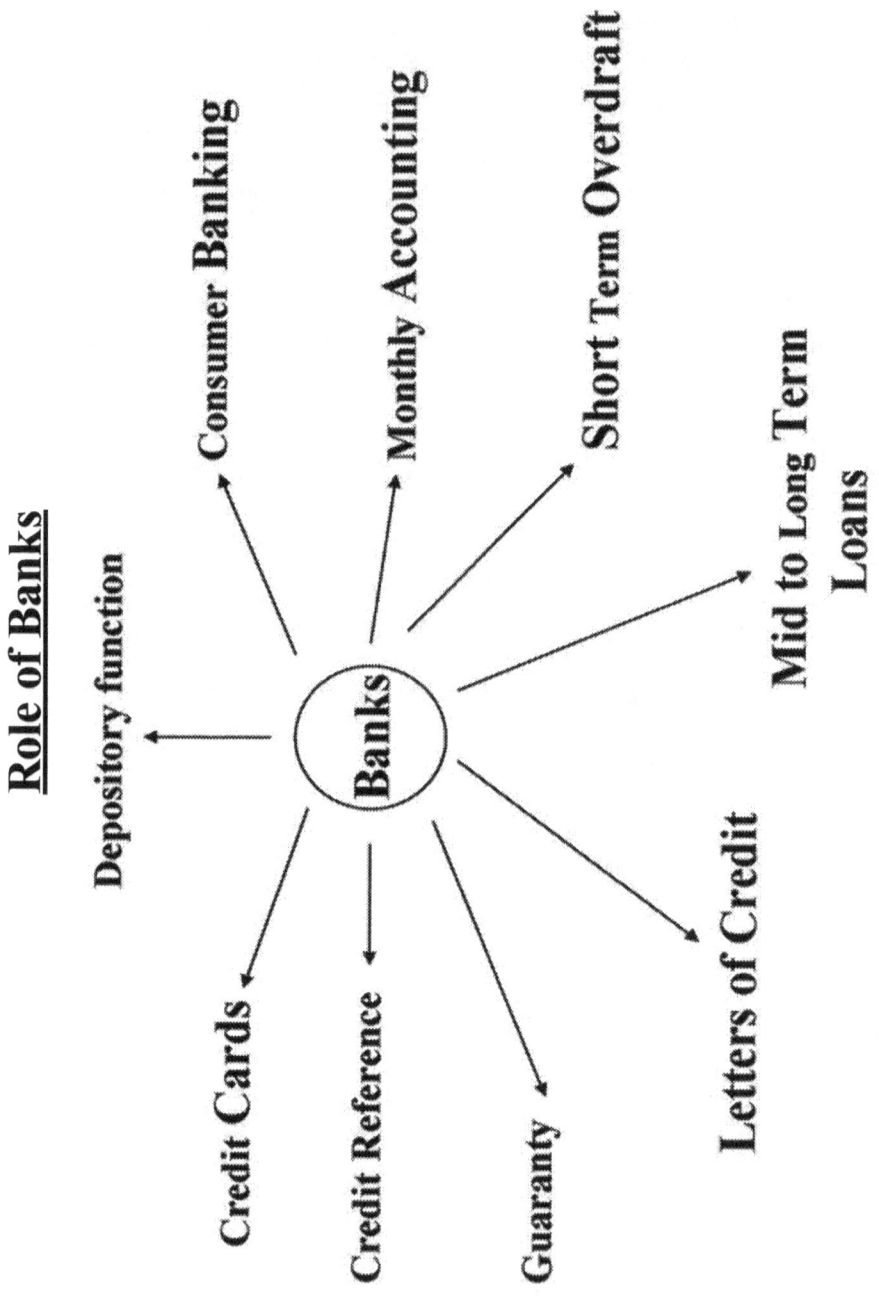

Role of Banks

Banks

- Consumer Banking
- Monthly Accounting
- Short Term Overdraft
- Mid to Long Term Loans
- Letters of Credit
- Depository function
- Credit Cards
- Credit Reference
- Guaranty

Chapter 8

How to Find the Right Bank for Your Needs

As mentioned earlier, you need to identify your needs and then find a bank that will satisfy those needs. Let us then start from a usual vanilla bank, which provides basic facilities.

Banks in general: Banking institutions are of many kinds. Some specialize in retail banking, while others specialize in commercial banking. Some put an emphasis on foreign banking operations, while others do only domestic transactions. Some are strong in understanding some of the industries well, like hotels, apartment complexes, and the oil and gas industry, while others would never touch them. Some are more conservative than others in almost all their affairs. Some emphasize savings and their products, while others are more sophisticated and handle many other portfolios. As mentioned earlier, the Glass-Steagall Act has remained one of the pillars of banking laws since its passage in 1933 by separating commercial banking and investment banking in general. However, since the relaxation of these laws by a recent supreme courts ruling, some involve themselves in insurance and securities, while others are still waiting on the sidelines either to acquire some experienced hands in these areas. Some are still looking at the risk and benefits of such activities, while others may have decided never to handle such business.

Out of all these different classes of banks, the entrepreneur has to fish out a right bank for himself and his future venture, which the bank that he has chosen is ready to support wholeheartedly.

Retail banking: In the U.S., private-unit banking at the street level has been the way banks have worked until recently. It is currently changing with mergers and acquisitions that are continuously taking place in this industry. Some predict there will be only mega banks in due course, created by the merger of many small banks.

We normally find small banks with assets of nearly $250 million on the rural and midsize towns of the U.S. They all deal with consumer banking and also satisfy the needs of borrowers for small businesses. Banks with $250 to $750 million in assets are midsize banks that again do the same things that small banks are doing. However, they tend to be more ready to seek lending opportunities with the right customers whose demands may not be met by the small banks, because of the limitations of their asset size and regulators' guidelines on their lending limits.

Banks with more than $750 million in assets are generally large banks. They are located in larger commercial cities and centers, but they may also have their presence in smaller towns through their branches. They will have all the departments that may satisfy your business and personal needs. These banks are probably the best bet if your needs are varied and if you need a multibranch-operation bank, or if you have some large component of your business involved in international transactions, and LCs.

As mentioned earlier, almost everyone has some banking relations for their needs. Most of the time you have a savings or a checking account in which you have some money in a positive balance. Banks like this kind of account very much. Banks look upon such accounts as a ready source for the short-term deposits, which the banks may use for lending, while usually not having to pay any interest for the deposits in current accounts. Over and above this, the banks also earn a lot of profit from the daily operations of these accounts by way of credit and debit charges. In fact, in such cases you are financing your bank's need for acquiring capital to be given to a borrower and earning some interest. One should also remember that the banks have their own overhead expenses also while providing such services.

However, when this relationship turns into financing your business it is a different matter altogether. Instead of you having a deposit with the bank, you are now asking the bank to let you have their depositor's money to finance your business operations or acquisitions. For a new businessman or an entrepreneur, the hassle of starting the new venture in itself is at times burdensome. On top of that, if he then has to go around borrowing money from banks, his entrepreneurial spirit is tested to its maximum. In particular, going around for the first time requesting a loan is a learning process in itself. One has to learn many of its disciplines, keeping in mind the requirements and limitations of the banks to provide such loans.

If it is a first-time experience and the borrower has to contact one or more bankers, it is not an easy matter. Some people are not cut out to do that very easily, while others, perhaps a smaller number, have an inborn gift to be comfortable in almost any circumstance. However, for all of us, it is true that if we know what to expect, we may be better prepared to face it. Hence, all of us who wish to have banking relationships need to know the internal workings and thinking of the bank and its different departments. Also we need to know what their strengths and weaknesses are, if any.

Bank's own strengths and weaknesses: Some banks have strengths in some businesses and industries, while they are not very keen on lending in others in which they do not possess enough experience. Like in any business, some banks are more comfortable dealing with one industry than the other, since they have better experience with a particular one. They all have money to lend, which is their primary business, and they make money by doing that.

However, to be comfortable in lending for a particular business, the bank would look internally to see if they have lending experience with that industry in the past. All businesses have different strengths and weaknesses, which eventually the lenders in such businesses start learning and making policies about. Conversely, different banks have their strengths in some businesses and industries backed by their past experience, while they do not have enough experience with other businesses.

For example, a bank that has been doing real estate loans may not want to be involved in nightclub operations, which they do not have experience in. Similarly, some of the businesses, like medical practice, have large receivables from insurance companies, which take a much longer time to materialize. Yet another type of operation may be businesses that deal only in cash, like fast-food chains, convenience stores, and the likes. Hence, the banks dealing in cash-flow retail businesses may find the medical practice's dealings with insurance receivables a bit too risky. Some of the banks love the medical-practice business, because they have a lot of experience in that line of business.

Such variations in the background of banks themselves make it very important to do some research as to which of the banks may be more poised to entertain your loan request out of the many available in town.

Chapter 9

Understanding Your Bank Thoroughly

To ensure a long-term, friendly, and beneficial relationship with your bank, you must understand certain facts. One of the most important, as mentioned earlier, is that banking is a business. In any business, it takes two parties to complete a transaction, which has to usually be beneficial to both. They may be a professional and his client or a service provider and his consumer. As in any business, both need each other. However, in free enterprises, in which the authorities promote competition, there are usually many alternatives available if you do not like one that you are dealing with. However, both parties must understand each other well and respect each other to make the relationship a success. It is no different in the bank and its customer relationship.

Banks look intimidating and aloof, but they are not: Bank usually have large and imposing building with wide corridors. Bankers almost always are dressed in dark suits and ties. The combination of this looks intimidating to many. For a novice, the nicely polished furniture and superb fixtures in a large and spacious bank building with formally dressed employees causes the immediate worry of trying and understanding where to start while asking for money.

However, you should not worry about these issues. You must remember that the bank needs you as much, if not more, than you need the bank. This is because it is their business to lend money, and if you are not there, they will have to find someone else to lend the same money to. This is how they make money and stay in business. You should perceive this no different than a supply-and-demand situation, which almost everyone has been exposed to in their school education and every day life. If the banks have got the money, on which they are paying interest to depositors, they must very quickly find a home for that money so that the bank may get a higher return than what they are paying. This is the only major way that the banks make their profits.

Let us try and understand this in a different way. Some of us have extra cash that we need to keep in safe place and at the same time earn some interest on it. Hence, we put it in the bank in a certificate of deposit (CD), money market account, or such similar instrument. The depositor may have kept that money for a certain period of time and expects it to be safe and increase in amount with interest earned. The bankers are the trustees of that money. That same money may travel from one to another borrower several times before the depositor is ready to pull it back. He is not concerned where that money has traveled in the meantime. He is only interested in the fact that his deposited amount remains safe and that he gets his deposit back with some interest earned. This is where the reputation of the bank comes in and gets built.

Banks are trustees and fiduciaries to their depositors: The bank cannot afford to make a tentative loan carrying a high risk and jeopardize the depositor's money. It is neither moral nor legal on the bank's part, since they are custodians and trustees, and it is their fiscal responsibility to ensure that the depositor's money is almost always safely placed.

We may try and look at the whole scenario in a different light. Banks are there to lend money as debt financing. Therefore, loss is usually never in their equation of loaning, except under unforeseen circumstances. They are only working as an intermediary for a depositor to find a home for their money where it will be well used and eventually returned with a reward in the shape of interest to the bank. By contrast, the equity investors, where the money may also be available, are ready to put their money at risk. They may win some, and the winning may be large, but they may then lose some also, which is never easily palatable to any bank.

Communication is the key: It is this aspect of banking that we are going to discuss at good length. It is the compliance aspect of servicing a loan by the borrower. If the borrower is not well informed, potential misunderstandings may be created. Hence, it is important that the borrower is in the know of his obligations to the lender. He may still not be able to comply with all the requirements of the lender, which, barring nonpayment, is usually not serious. Once in a while, even late payments or nonpayment due to some genuine cause may be condoned by sitting across the table and rescheduling the payment plans. However, this is only possible if the borrower tells the lender in good time that such a possibility is arising.

Hence, to keep everything in order there should be good communication between the borrower and the lender. If there is any issue of noncompliance, it should be rectified in good time. If it is not done with mutual understanding and negotiation, the relationship may break down. This may be serious for a business, since the relationship with banks is an important part of the whole equation in any business. A business cannot afford to let the bankers be turned from a friend to an adversary. It is bad for the business' reputation, so much so that the business may never be able to recuperate from its ill effects, causing it to be damaged permanently or even sometimes get closed down.

Conversely, though, the bank would not mind a late payment once in awhile instead of having a total nonpayment and the loan going bad. In fact, your loan officer may go out of his way to assist you under such circumstances to stay afloat and pay your loan with rescheduling. Hence, an open line of communication is an important factor in you having a fruitful and beneficial relationship with your bankers.

Specialties of lenders: Most of the banks do not indulge in lending any and all projects. Although they diversify their loan portfolio as best as possible, they have certain businesses that they like and others they do not. It is therefore of utmost importance that you do the necessary research and due diligence as to which of the lending institutions will suit you most. At times, you do not have a choice at all, because in rural areas or small towns there may be only one bank. In that case, you may get in touch with the right person and ask pertinent questions.

You may perhaps draw a corollary for going on a date or getting married. You want to make sure of your partner's strengths or weaknesses before proposing your loan. (It is, in fact, called a proposal, probably for the same reason.) You will want to know in what, if any, particular area the bank is experienced and keen to lend. You will specifically want to know if the bank is comfortable in lending your kind of business. This is all because, as mentioned earlier, all banks do not feel comfortable lending money in some of the sectors of industry or businesses that they do not have experience in. If they do not have the faintest idea of the intricacies of your business, the bank will not be comfortable lending to you.

Again, it comes to a repetition of the first principle. Banks are trustees of someone else's deposits, and they have a fiduciary responsibility to ensure that they do not lend deposits in businesses that may be risky or that they do not have much knowledge about. It is a long-term relationship in which the bank would want to be on top of things in inspecting and examining your reports and understanding them on a regular basis.

References and formalities: It would be better to have someone refer you to the banker, and the best reference could be your attorney or accountant. They generally know the local banks well enough to recommend you to go to the right one for your needs. You must make an appointment to see the person and be presentable. It is also important not to be intimidated. As mentioned earlier, the relationship is mutually beneficial for both parties, as in any business. Customarily, the bankers remain formal, true to their tradition in the banking business.

Banks are businesses: However, behind their formal blue or black suits and nice neckties they are really looking for and are actually on a hunt for a person like you. They need to have a person or a company with good references. The bankers are looking for someone with experience to handle money with care and have past history of returning the debts. They would love to lend to such a person even if he may be a beginner in a new business.

They are looking for a trustworthy party with some good references and good past credit history so that they do not have to worry about the repayment of the loan or its going bad. Particularly if banks have large deposits and if their loan portfolio is comparatively small, they may be almost desperate to find someone who is dependable and reputable. Although it may sound repetitive, it is important to understand that bankers are human beings like us and are in need of someone like us needing to borrow and then return the loan with its interest on time, without causing any worry or sleepless nights over it.

Remember that you are a customer for the banking business, and usually for most businesses, the customer is always right! So long as you do not take an unfair advantage of your position, the bank also would not mind treating you so.

Chapter 10

Having a Formal Meeting with Your Banker

The meeting: Say you have identified, through your due diligence a bank that you think, according to your information, may be ready to lend money in the kind of business that you want to start. Now you need to meet the banker in person. You need to get an appointment and be there on time. Remember, the first impression is important, so help yourself to create the best one on that day. You may have gathered some information on the bank and the loan officer already, which will help you to position yourself in your meeting with the banker.

Your banker's impression about you: However, try and understand one very simple thing: when you are meeting your banker for the first time, he does not know anything about you. Your introduction may have been through some good friend's reference, for example from your CPA or attorney. Keep in mind that your banker does not know much about you. Hence, he needs to create your picture in his mind, not only about your business, but also about you in general. This may include a lot of business-related activities as well as about yourself personally. It may include matters like where you live, what your social life is like, what your views are about many things in general, and even an informal discussion about your family and friends. On your part, you need to ensure that your banker develops a confidence about you and your ability to conduct your business in a most professional manner, which, in turn, will tell him that his loan is safe and will be repaid without any difficulty.

It may not be quite legal for the banker to be very intrusive in your personal life or your philosophical or political views, but then he has a responsibility to predict how good a paymaster you would be of the money that they might lend you. This is tantamount to what we may term as "future reading" about you on your banker's part. He has to do this without a crystal ball and, hence, he needs as much information about you as possible, relevant or even non-relevant. He then has such information analyzed with relevance to your ability and even intention to pay back the loan that he would consider extending to you. Your bankers do it every day, and that is what he has been trained for.

Define your borrowing needs: To be able to present an appropriate proposal to the lending agency, you first need to define your own need to know what the type of loan is that will suit your requirements. That is the only way you will be able to spell out your needs correctly to your would-be financier.

This requires some advice and hand holding by one of your mentors. It may seem like trying to have preliminary lessons about banks and their work. Yet, it is important for you to learn and find out what are the different kinds of loans that the bank provides and the difference between them. This knowledge will arm you to discuss your options with your banker more meaningfully and intelligently. It is this discussion and other meetings through which the banker will assess you and your understanding not only about your business but also about the world of finances and money, into which you are about to wet your feet by starting to borrow. Through these meetings the banker will develop an impression about you, as to how knowledgeable you are about banking, borrowing, and perhaps about the responsibility that you are about to undertake to repay the loan that you might be approved for.

Anyway, talking about the type of loans, we have already discussed the facilities that the banking institutions may offer. You need to discuss your need with your banker to arrive at the correct type of financing that will suit your needs. For example, as discussed elsewhere, between you and your banker, you must decide whether it is a seasonal need in your business that needs a larger capital around a particular time of the year. In such a case, you should ensure that the maturity of loan is sometime after the season is over and you have received your cash back to comfortably repay your obligations. You may also be in need of a cyclical need of cash flow or regular working capital. Each will have to be tailor-made for you to ensure that the repayment is on time without any hitch.

Some general conversation topics about current issues: You may also want to discuss current economic issues with your banker. Usually they are quite up to date with such things with most current possible news about the strength of currency, balance of payments, unemployment rate and the like. Your discussion will also indicate to him about your understanding of current economic situations, which probably will have a lot of bearing on the success or otherwise of your business. Your knowledge about these issues will also comfort the banker that you are mindful of these issues and their impact on your business, in particular, and national economic health, in general. While discussing such generic, yet important day-to-day issues, you should be knowledgeable about at least the correct recent and comparative past reports about the subject under discussion so as not to cut a sorry figure. Not having enough exposure to such matters may create a negative impression at the start, which must be avoided.

Banks are not pawn shops: It must be remembered that the banks would surely require collateral for the loan. However they are not lenders on the strength of the collateral, as the pawn shops are. Banks would look at the character of the borrower and his repayment capacity from the primary source of profit generation for which the loan has been created. Collateral and a guaranty are only secondary sources in the eyes of the banker. Hence, if you are asking for a loan from a seasoned banker on the strength of collateral, you may be surprised that it may not be entertained as easily as it would be on your own personal strength as the main support for loan creation.

Chapter 11
Small Business Administration (SBA)

Conventional banks are very conservative by nature in taking any unusual risks. In such circumstances, in the past few years the SBA has been aggressive in the lending market to help the economy by helping small businesses obtain necessary capital. Usually, the small businesses are considered to be a larger risk by conservative bankers. The reason of such thinking is the fact that a substantial number of new businesses fail to survive a long time. It is said that only one in five (20% only) new businesses and corporations survive to see the fifth year of its life, meaning four of the five close down. This is an almost nightmarish figure for conservative bankers. However, the government would like to promote the entrepreneurs. Hence, they have been pushing programs to assist the entrepreneurs to obtain the much-needed capital from the street bank, which is guaranteed by the SBA and, hence, the exposure of risk to the bank is reduced.

History of the SBA:

Largely as a response to the pressures of the Great Depression and World War II, President Herbert Hoover created the Reconstruction Finance Corporation (RFC) in 1932 to alleviate the financial crisis of the Great Depression, which was the SBA's ancestor. The RFC was basically a federal lending program for all businesses hurt by the Depression, large and small. It was adopted as the personal project of Hoover's successor, President Franklin D. Roosevelt.

Concern for small businesses intensified during World War II, when large industries beefed up production to accommodate wartime defense contracts, and smaller businesses were left unable to compete. To help small businesses participate in war production and give them financial viability, Congress created the Smaller War Plants Corporation (SWPC) in 1942. The SWPC provided direct loans to private entrepreneurs and encouraged large financial institutions to make credit available to small enterprises. The SWPC advocated on behalf of small-business interests to federal procurement agencies and big businesses also.

The SWPC was dissolved after the war, and its lending and contract powers were handed over to the RFC. At this time, the Office of Small Business (OSB) in the Department of Commerce also assumed some responsibilities that would later become characteristic duties of the SBA. Its services were primarily educational. Believing that a lack of information and expertise was the main cause of small-business failure, the OSB produced training brochures and conducted management counseling for individual entrepreneurs.

Congress created another wartime organization to handle small-business concerns during the Korean War, this time called the Small Defense Plants Administration (SDPA). Its functions were similar to those of the SWPC, except that ultimate lending authority was retained by the RFC. The SDPA certified small businesses to the RFC when it had determined the businesses to be competent to perform the work of government contracts.

President Dwight Eisenhower proposed creation of a new small-business agency in 1952. The U.S. Small Business Administration (SBA) was created by the Small Business Act of July 30, 1953. Its function was to "aid, counsel, assist, and protect, insofar as is possible, the interests of small business concerns." The charter also stipulated that the SBA would ensure small businesses a "fair proportion" of government contracts and sales of surplus property.

By 1954, the SBA already was making direct business loans and guarantying bank loans to small businesses. The SBA was also making loans to victims of natural disasters, working to get government procurement contracts for small businesses, and helping business owners with management, technical assistance, and business training.

The Investment Company Act of 1958 established the Small Business Investment Company (SBIC) Program, under which SBA licensed, regulated, and helped provide funds for privately owned and operated venture capital investment firms. They specialized in providing long-term debt and equity investments to high-risk small businesses. Its creation was the result of a Federal Reserve study that discovered, in the simplest terms, that small businesses could not get the credit they needed to keep pace with technological advancement.

The SBA created the Equal Opportunity Loan (EOL) Program in 1964. The EOL Program relaxed the credit and collateral requirements for applicants living below the poverty level in an effort to encourage new businesses. The EOL particularly helped those sound commercial initiatives that had been unable to get financial backing from usual sources.

Since its inception, the SBA has grown in terms of total assistance provided and has created an array of programs tailored to encourage small enterprises in all areas. The SBA's programs now include financial and federal contract-procurement assistance, management assistance, and specialized outreach to women, minorities, and armed forces veterans. The SBA also provides loans to victims of natural disasters and specialized advice and assistance in international trade.

Nearly twenty million small businesses have received direct or indirect help from one or another of those SBA programs since 1953, as the agency has become the government's most cost-effective instrument for economic development. Over the past decade (1991–2000), the SBA has helped almost 435,000 small businesses get more than $94.6 billion in loans, more than in the entire history of the agency before 1991. Since 1958, the SBA's venture-capital program has put more than $30 billion into the hands of small business owners to finance their growth. In the year 2001, the SBA backed more than $12.3 billion in loans to small businesses. More than $1 billion was made available for disaster loans and more than $40 billion in federal contracts were secured by small businesses with the SBA's help.

The SBA continues to branch out to increase business participation by women and minorities along new avenues, such as the minority small business program and micro loans.

Summary of Chapter 11

<u>Evolution of SBA</u>

• 1932: After Depression President Herbert Hoover creates Reconstruction Finance Corporation (RFC)

• 1942: Smaller War Plants Corporation (SWPC) created by Congress.

• Office of Small Business (OSB) in the department of Commerce starts economic activities and assistance.

• Korean War: Congress created Small Defense Plants Administration (SDPA)

• 1953: President Eisenhower creates the SBA.

• 1954: SBA becomes active.

• 1958: Small Business Investment Company (SBIC) created.

• 1964: Equal Opportunity Loan program (EOL) created within the SBA.

Chapter 12
Various SBA Loan Programs

The SBA offers a variety of financing options and loan programs for small businesses. The SBA's assistance usually is in the form of loan guarantees. This means that the SBA guarantees loans made by banks and other private lenders to small-business clients.

THE SBA'S BASIC PROGRAM 7(A) LOAN GUARANTY PROGRAM: The 7(a) loans are the most basic and most used type of the SBA's business loan programs. Its name comes from section 7(a) of the Small Business Act, which authorizes the agency to provide business loans to small businesses. All 7(a) loans that the SBA guarantees must meet prescribed criteria. The business gets a loan from its lender with a 7(a) structure, and the lender gets a SBA guaranty on a portion or percentage of this loan. Consequently, the primary business-loan-assistance program available to small business from the SBA is called the 7(a) guaranty loan program.

Objective: This serves as the SBA's primary business loan program to help qualified small businesses obtain financing when they might not be eligible for business loans through normal lending channels. It is also the agency's most flexible business-loan program, since financing under this program can be guaranteed for a variety of general business purposes.

Usage: Loan proceeds can be used for most sound business purposes. These include working capital, machinery and equipment, furniture and fixtures, land and building (including purchase, renovation, and new construction), and leasehold improvements. Loan amortization is long. Presently, it is up to ten years for working capital and generally up to twenty-five years for fixed assets.

Disbursement: All 7(a) loans are disbursed through commercial lending institutions, which are called participants because they participate with the SBA in the 7(a) program. Not all lenders choose to participate, but most banks do. There are also some nonbank lenders who participate with the SBA in the 7(a) program, which expands the availability of lenders making loans under SBA guidelines.

Guaranty: These 7(a) loans are only available on a guaranty basis. This means they are provided by lenders who choose to structure their own loans by the SBA's requirements and who apply and receive a guaranty from the SBA on a portion of this loan. The SBA does not fully guaranty 7(a) loans. The lender and the SBA share the overall risk if a borrower is not able to repay the loan in full. The guaranty is for payment default only and does not cover imprudent decisions by the lender or misrepresentation by the borrower.

Procedure: Under the guaranty concept, commercial lenders make and administer the loans. The business owner applies to an approved lender for their financing. The lender will decide if they will make the loan internally as a conventional loan. However, if the lender is not comfortable with the risk but still thinks that the loan is justified in the interest of the business promotion, they will reduce their risk by requesting the SBA guaranty if the loan is to be made. The guaranty, which the SBA provides, is only available to the lender. It assures the lender that in the event the borrower does not repay their obligation and payment default occurs, the government will reimburse the lender for its loss, up to the percentage of the SBA's guaranty. Under this program, the borrower remains obligated for the full amount due.

Actual lender: A key concept of the 7(a) guaranty loan program is that the loan actually comes from a commercial lender, not the government. If the lender is not willing to provide the loan, even if they may be able to get a SBA guaranty, the agency cannot force the lender to change their mind. Neither can the SBA make the loan by itself, because the agency does not lend the actual physical money. Therefore, it is paramount that all applicants positively approach the lender for a loan and that they know the lender's criteria and requirements as well as those of the SBA. In order to obtain positive consideration for an SBA-supported loan, the applicant must be both eligible and creditworthy.

Repayment from an SBA-financed business: In order to get a 7(a) loan, the applicant must first be eligible. The most primary consideration in the SBA loan decision process is an ability to repay the loan from the cash flow of the business itself. However, other important conditions are good character, management capability, valuable collateral, and owner's equity contribution. All owners of 20% or more shares or stocks are also required to personally guarantee SBA loans.

Eligibility criteria: All applicants must be eligible to meet criteria to be considered for a 7(a) loan. However, eligibility requirements are designed to be as broad as possible in order that this lending program can accommodate the most diverse variety of small-business financing needs. All businesses that are considered for financing under the SBA's 7(a) loan program must meet SBA size standards, and be able to demonstrate repayment capability. Certain variations of the SBA's 7(a) loan program may also require some additional eligibility criteria. Special-purpose programs also identify some additional criteria.

Character considerations: The SBA must determine if the principals of each applicant firm have historically shown the willingness and ability to pay their debts and that they are law-abiding. The agency must know if there are any factors that have an impact on these issues. Therefore, a Statement of Personal History is obtained from each principal. Hence, in theory, the applicants must at least have a good credit history and should meet the requisite rules and guidelines of the SBA.

Other aspects of the 7(a) loan program: In addition to credit and eligibility criteria, an applicant should be aware of the general types of terms and conditions they can expect if the SBA is involved in the financial assistance. The specific terms of SBA loans are negotiated between an applicant and the participating financial institution, subject to the requirements of the SBA.

Upper ceiling of the lending under the SBA: Maximum loan amounts for the SBA are fixed, and the SBA guaranty is a percentage of that amount, which will be lower if the loan amount is lesser than maximum allowed.

SBA guaranty fees: There is also a fixed loan fee for the SBA loans, which the agency charges for the guaranty that it supplies to the lending institution on behalf of the borrower. This fee sometimes makes the SBA loan less attractive and more expensive for the borrower. On the other hand, that needs to be weighed against its long-term benefits and other preferable terms, like a fixed interest rate in some of the programs and a longer amortization in others.

Prepayment penalty: Another condition, which needs to be considered seriously by the borrower, is the prepayment penalty clause, which is in most of the SBA loans and may be considered as a hurdle if the borrower wishes to have an early exit from that venture.

Long maturity terms: Maturity terms for 7(a) loans are generally with longer amortization, giving the entrepreneur a stable long-term situation of cash flow. This is a big plus point for the SBA-guaranteed loan, since the conventional bank loan will usually have a five- or seven-year balloon with an amortization of ten to fifteen years.

There are several other programs of the SBA, which may be useful in different circumstances to the businessman and the entrepreneur. We shall describe some of those here.

THE SBA'S LOAN PREQUALIFICATION PROGRAM: This program is designed to expedite smaller loan applications, which are first sanctioned by the SBA, and then the approval or commitment letter is provided to the lending institution.

Objective: This allows business applicants to have their loan applications for $250,000 or less analyzed and potentially sanctioned by the SBA before they are taken to lenders for consideration. The program focuses on the applicant's character, credit, experience, and reliability. An SBA-designated intermediary works with the business owner to review and strengthen the loan application. The review is based on key financial ratios and the credit and business history of principal owners. The SBA's Office of Field Operations and SBA district office supervise this program. This is very useful and suitable for designated small businesses.

Intermediaries: This prequalification program is administered through nonprofit intermediaries such as Small Business Development Centers (SBDC) and Certified Development Companies (CDC) operating in specific geographic areas. These intermediaries assist prospective borrowers in developing viable loan application packages and securing loans. This program targets low-income borrowers, disabled business owners, new and emerging businesses, veterans, exporters, and rural and specialized industries.

Procedure: The job of the intermediary is to work with the applicant to make sure the business plan is complete and that the application is both eligible and has credit merit. If the intermediary is satisfied that the application has a chance for approval, it will send it to the SBA for processing. Small Business Development Centers serving as intermediaries do not charge a fee for loan packaging. Once the loan package is assembled, it is submitted to the SBA for expedited consideration. The SBA conducts a thorough analysis of the case. It uses the same criteria for degree of analysis within the similar timeframe.

Commitment letter: If the SBA decides the application is eligible and has sufficient credit merit to warrant approval, it will issue a commitment letter. The commitment letter, or prequalification letter, indicates the SBA's willingness to guaranty a loan made by a lender under certain terms and conditions. The intermediary then helps the borrower locate a lender offering the most competitive services and rates. The applicant then takes the letter and its application documents to a lender for disbursement of actual loan proceeds.

Some specifics of the prequalification program: The maximum loan amount for this pilot program is presently $250,000. Interest rates, maturities, collateral policies, and guaranty percentages, are the same as the standard 7(a) loan program.

THE SBA'S MICRO LOAN, A 7(M) LOAN PROGRAM: This program, as its name suggests, is for very small loans.

Objective: Provides short-term loans of up to $35,000 to small businesses and not-for-profit child-care centers for working capital or the purchase of inventory, supplies, furniture, fixtures, machinery, and/or equipment. Proceeds cannot be used to pay existing debts or to purchase real estate. The SBA makes or guarantees a loan to an intermediary, who in turn makes the micro loan to the applicant. These organizations also provide management and technical assistance. The micro loan program is available in selected locations in most states. This program is suitable for small-scale financing and technical assistance for start-up or expansion.

This program is administered through specially designated intermediary lenders, who are nonprofit organizations with experience in lending and in technical assistance.

THE SBA'S 504 LOAN PROGRAM THROUGH CERTIFIED DEVELOPMENT COMPANY (CDC): This program allows for a higher amount of SBA loan guaranty for use in real estate projects.

Objective: This program provides long-term, fixed-rate financing to small businesses to acquire real estate, machinery, and equipment, and for expansion and/or modernization. Typically, a 504 project includes a loan secured from a private-sector lender with a senior lien, a loan secured from a CDC (funded by a 100% SBA-guaranteed debenture). Junior liens cover up to 40% of the total cost, and usually require a contribution of at least 10% equity from the borrower. Presently, the maximum SBA debenture limit is $1 million (and up to $1.3 million in some cases).

This is suitable for small businesses requiring brick-and-mortar financing. This is administered through CDCs, which are private, nonprofit corporations set up to contribute to the economic development of their communities or regions.

Summary of Chapter 12

<u>SBA Loan Programs</u>

- SBA 7(a) Loan guaranty program.

- Loan Pre-qualification program by Small Business Development Centers (SBDC) and Certified Development Companies (CDC.)

- SBA 7(m) Micro loan program.

- SBA 504 Loan Program through CDC

Chapter 13
How to Write a Loan Proposal

Preliminary to loan application: In essence, the loan application is nothing more than the presentation of all facts about your proposed business with your expected projection of the same. Hence, your first step would be to discuss your loan needs informally with your banker. Once he feels some initial comfort that the loan request could possibly be looked upon seriously by the loan committee, he will request that you provide him with your loan application in writing. You should provide the lender with your loan application with as much relevant information as possible, as discussed at length in previous chapters.

Initial scrutiny of loan application: You must also provide some of the pertinent supportive documents to support the loan application. Having done that, in the next meeting or during a telephone visit, you need to know how the loan officer perceives your application and what the chances are of its approval. If all is well, he will let you know that you stand a good chance to at least be accepted for preliminary examination. You will usually have an informal reply to your application within about ten days indicating whether or not your application stands a good chance to be approved.

Commitment letter: At the end of that initial assessment, if the lender still thinks your application has a fair chance to be approved, they will give you a nonbinding commitment letter with broad terms and conditions and interest rates. This means that your application falls within the framework of their loaning criteria. However, this will be a provisional commitment letter and will be subject to the application meeting all their criteria. The real processing of your application starts from there on in detail, provided you agree in principle with their initial terms and conditions. You will need to return the commitment letter duly signed for them to start this processing.

Proposal is the key: The proposal of loan is the most important stage for your business and for your future relationship with your bank and lender. Since apart from perhaps a cursory meeting that you may have had with your lender, he does not know much about you, making this the right time for you to provide all the pertinent information about you and your business in as much detail as possible. The more comfortable the lender is with you and your proposal, the quicker you will have the necessary loan released to you for you to be on your way to realize your dreams.

Your presentation: As we know in everyday life, the presentation is all too important. The same is true for loan proposals also. You need to present the proposal in such a way that it makes out a case for your own proposal in front of the lender on your behalf. Again, you must look at your proposal from the perspective of the lender for you to understand the important elements that you need to include in it and how it may be presented and highlighted. It is all a matter of common sense and logic. It may be difficult on the first occasion, when you may need to ask for advice from someone who has done it before. However, once you have done it, it becomes a matter of routine thereafter.

Approval of your loan request depends on how well you present yourself, your business, and your financial needs to a lender. Remember, lenders want to make loans, since they are in the business of lending, and are looking for good prospects to lend to. However, they will make loans only if, according to their crystal-ball future-telling coupled with some specific calculations, the lender is led to think that the loan will be repaid as agreed.

The best way to improve your chances of obtaining a loan is to prepare a detailed written proposal. This should include all the relevant information that the lender would like to know. The lenders form their decision for any loan proposal by considering the facts of the business, its profitability, and who the people behind the business entity or organization are. On the basis of such particulars they conclude if this loan will almost certainly be good and repaid as agreed. They would also like to be comfortable with the fact that if the business gets into problems there is a strong enough secondary source to support the loan. For your loan application to be successful, your written loan proposal should include the following details.

General information: You need to start with the general information about yourself and your business. This includes as much detail as possible, like business name, names of principals, social security number for each principal, and the business address. You need to specify the amount needed, as exact as possible, and justify that requirement with some backup papers. This may include the cost of machinery, improvements, quotations, cash-flow projections and other relevant information. You should include the purpose of the loan in exact terms to illustrate what the loan will be used for and why it is needed. The lender would like to know the specific use of the funds being provided to you. This is because they would like you to use the funds in that specific business. The lender would not allow you to invest the loan proceeds in some other business, pay some previous debt with it, or pilfer the same. The lender's worry would be that such alternative use will seriously preclude the possibility of the repayment of the loan.

Business description: You should provide in detail the history and nature of the business. Details may include the kind of business it is, its age, number of employees, and current business assets.

Legal entity's structure: You will also need to provide the lender the ownership structure of the entity seeking the loan. This should include details about your company's legal structure and whether it is a limited-liability entity, partnership, or proprietorship concern. If the business is run as a legal entity, which is a limited-liability corporation, partnership, or company, an organogram showing the management and control structure of the entity must be provided. If it is a proprietorship or partnership business, it should be explained as to who are the principals.

Management Profile: Management is the most important element assessed by money lenders. Describe briefly the role of each of the principals in your business. Also provide their background, business experience, education experience, skills, and accomplishments. This may be in the shape of resumes of the important personnel in the organization.

Market information: You must clearly define your company's products as well as your market. Describe the main competitors and how will you be able to withstand the competition of the existing businesses. Also provide a description and profile of your customers and explain how your business can satisfy their needs.

Financial information: You need to include your most current financial statement, which consists of balance sheets and income statements. Also include the same information for the past three years, if the business is that old. If you are starting out, provide a projected balance sheet and income statement. You also need to provide the personal financial statements on yourself and other principal owners of the business. An important thing about the personal information will be your cash-flow statement of the past and projected year. Also mention the collateral you are willing to pledge as security for the loan and its approximate value.

Your equity participation: The lender would like to ensure and see that you have enough equity stakes in the business that you wish to be financed. They would usually be comfortable if your equity in the project is, say, more than 20% of the total cost of the project. Remember, no lender or investor will finance 100% of your business. However, as a rule of thumb, unless the business is of some unusual nature, the lenders would be generally satisfied to see about 20% to 30% of the project as your equity, and they will lend the balance value of the project. However, these are only general guidelines. The lender weighs each project individually on its own merits. They may finance one project with as little as 10% of your equity, while they may not finance other project with even 50% equity. This decision is quite subjective on some occasions and is dependent on the comfort level that the lender finds in you with regards to the repayment of the loan.

Your experience and resume: The lender would like to see if you have sufficient experience and training to operate a successful business. This is because your repaying capacity will depend on the success of the business, which in turn will depend on the experience that you have in that business. Hence, it will be prudent for you to include your resume, stressing the strengths that you have acquired through long enough experience in the field of business that you wish to pursue.

Business plan: You should give as much detail as possible, which may show that you have a good business plan that demonstrates your understanding of and commitment to the success of the business. All the above information with necessary projections is called a business plan. If it is convincing, the lender will have no problem giving you a positive reply to your application.

Cash flow and loan repayment projections: You need to give the lender a three years' cash-flow projection for them to be comfortable to lend you the amount that you need for the business. They would like to know that you would not need any further cash from the lender to meet your obligations. The lender would like to ascertain that REPAYMENT OF YOUR LOAN OBLIGATIONS WILL BE PRIMARILY PAID FROM THE PROFITS OF YOUR BUSINESS. Again, this is for the lender to ensure that in case of difficulty with the loan, the other strengths that you have demonstrated, like collateral and the principal's cash flow, are in reserve for them to fall back on.

Loan packaging service: A large number of accountants, former bank loan officers, and people with knowledge of borrowing and lending provide this service at reasonable fees. This includes creating a loan package, which may cover all the relevant information needed by the lender. Some of these people know the idiosyncrasies of certain lenders, and, hence, may be able to present the package in such a way that it will attract the attention of the lender more so than otherwise. This is worth considering if you are not quite experienced with such a presentation.

Packaging help from Service Corps of Retired Executives (SCORE) and Small Business Development Centers (SBDC): SCORE and SBDC may be the best and free help for, in particular, entrepreneurs requiring SBA loans. Their addresses in most cities may be obtained from a local SBA office. They are well conversant to work with small businesses and are free resources for the borrower, since they are supported by the SBA.

Summary of Chapter 13

Components of Your Loan Application

Loan application

- General info about you and your business
- Management profile of business
- Market information
- Financial information
- Legal structure of business entity
- Your experience and resume
- Business plan
- Cash flow for 3 years
- Loan packaging

Chapter 14
How to Successfully Qualify for a Loan

The lender will lend only if it is safe to do so: When you apply for a loan, the bank will need you to support your application with information and documentary evidence. The lender's reason for asking for such supporting documents is simple. They want to ensure and be certain that the loan that they are considering giving will be safe in your hands and that it will be repaid as per the terms and conditions with interest. Yet another aspect that the bank will want to look at is that the payment will be possible from the business activities and its profits and not from other sources. It is only in some unforeseen eventuality that they rely on making good on their loaned money through collateral or guarantees that you have offered.

Lenders are hungry for information: First of all, let us understand why banks would want all this information. Before the bank parts with their money and gives it to you, their main concern is whether or not you will pay their money back as per the plan and agreement. They are playing a predictability game on your ability for repayment on the basis of the information that you will provide and the information that they have collected on you and your industry. Once they are satisfied on this point, they would like to have a fallback plan also. In case you cannot pay the obligation, they want to know how they can recover their money from your business, its assets, or other collateral that they may have asked you to pledge. The bank will also like to see a substantial equity commitment from you as down payment. It may be anything from 10% to 50% of the project cost, depending upon many other factors.

Once you have understood the objective of the exercise, the formalities will be all meaningful to you, and it will be possible for you to stay a step ahead of the requirements of the lender. Typically, almost all the documents in the following list will be relevant to support your loan application with. Hence, you will need to provide almost all and perhaps some more details and documents from the list described below:

Business plan: We have discussed this in the last chapter. This is the plan that you have been dreaming about, which you have now written on paper as a business plan. This would also includes many other documents like your financial statements, you and your company's IRS returns for three years, your cash-flow projections for the business, and personal cash flow.

This is the first set of documents that you are likely to provide to the bank. It may be during a verbal chat in your first meeting when you will explain your plan and why you will need the bank's assistance to fulfill that plan. The bank will desire that you put this plan in a formal written application indicating some of the salient features pertaining to you, your business organization, and industry.

You should prepare this in detail. It should include the historical data of your business if it is an ongoing business. It may include the history of the industry or line of business that you are pursuing. This should also include short resumes of the personnel that you have or will hire with their qualifications and experience. You will include here some information about the competitors and how well they are doing. Banks will want to see at least a three-year projection of your cash flow to see that you will be liquid enough to be able to repay the loan that you are taking.

IRS returns: A new business would not have the IRS return yet, but for an old and ongoing business the bank would like to see three years of IRS returns to see that you have been profitable or showing such a trend. This is for them to predict your future and, hence, their loan's security. The returns may also have to be confirmed with the tax department to ensure that they were the returns actually submitted.

Financial statements: The bank would like to see the financial statement of the business if it is ongoing. If it is a new business, they will want to see your own financials to see the net worth of the owners or officers. The bank will probably ask for the financials and cash-flow projections of all the shareholders with a 20% or more stake in the business. This is to ensure that the bank is lending to people of sizeable net worth and that in case of difficulty, there may be other avenues to make good the loan payments.

Balance sheet: This is another tool that will indicate to the lenders that in an existing business there is adequate capital and net worth. It will also show them that you are making profit, which eventually shows on the balance sheet. Balance sheet will also consist of all the information, from which the lender may deduce the ratios of assets and liabilities that they will be interested in to approve the loan.

Cash flow: This is considered to be the most important tool by many seasoned bankers to assess the liquidity and, hence, ability to pay back the loan. You will repay the loan comfortably only if you have a positive cash flow. This may be required for the existing business and for the principals of the business.

Collateral: This is an interesting issue. The person or business offering a piece of real estate or equipment may consider it to be very valuable. However, the bank's perspective is entirely different on the valuation of collateral. The bank will look upon that as a last resort for making good on the loan in case of difficulty in repayment. As mentioned earlier, banks are in the business of "renting the use" the money and not in business of acquiring the real estate and equipment and then selling it to make good on the loan that has gone bad. Therefore, however valuable the asset may be, they will always discount that value by some percentage points. This is to create a comfort zone for the lender, so as not to make a loss on the loan if they actually have to sell the collateral, which may not be sold at its real worth for any number of reasons. This discount, which usually varies according to the type of collateral, is a subjective decision that takes into account many other factors in the loan application.

In general, one may say that the lenders would wish to have all their loan dollars covered by some sound collateral, which may not happen in practical life. However, if the lender can get a higher value collateral, he would prefer doing so and, hence, how much collateral to offer and pledge is a matter to be decided by mutual agreement and negotiation.

Appraisal of collateral assets: Once you have identified acceptable collateral to pledge against in support of your loan application, the bank will need to get it appraised. The lender will not leave anything to chance. They will typically hire a professional third-party appraisal company to ensure that they have sound, good, and valuable collateral verified by the appraiser. Professional appraisal is expensive and, hence, it is ordered after it has been agreed in principle that the bank will offer the requested loan if the appraisal of the asset is what they would like to see to be able to support the requested loan amount. In other words, the loan amount is a percentage of the value of the collateral. This percentage is not quite fixed, and different banks may offer a higher or lower percentage of the value, depending upon how comfortable they feel with other factors in the business plan that they are looking at to finally offer the loan amount.

Environmental report: If you are pledging a property, the bank would like it inspected by a professional third-party environmental company. They will order an environmental report on the immovable property you have proposed as collateral. The cost of such report has to be usually borne by the loan applicant. The bank would like to see that the asset offered as pledge is clean and free from any pollutants, which might reduce its value or will require a large sum of money to clean it. This report will tell them that the collateralized property is safe and sound for them to fall back on if the loan does not get paid as planned.

Receivables of your business with aging analysis: Again, the objective here is to see that your receivables are currently in line with the industry practice that you are in. Banks may accept the receivables as collateral and, hence, they would be very interested in its soundness, or that they are all collectible and will not turn into bad debts. If the receivables are the collateral, the bank would like to see the aging analysis of that. This will tell them how good the receivables are in the industry you are working in. Usually, in most of the businesses where a credit is offered to customers, the payment terms are anything from ten to thirty days, while in some it may be as long as sixty or even ninety days. If your aging analysis shows the receivables to be older than the usual industry practice, the bank may not want to consider a portion of it as good collateral. Therefore, the percentage that they may offer as a loan against the receivable may drop. Typically, the amount of loan offered may be anything from 70%, down to 50%. It is also negotiable considering other factors on which the loan offering is based.

List of your assets and liabilities: As mentioned earlier, the bank would want to know everything about the business. There are some mathematical calculations with which they will determine whether or not your ratio of assets to liabilities is within their comfort level to extend your requested loan. Hence, they will also want to know what other liabilities that you have on the business to assess the health of your business. In fact, they will also want an assurance from you, which will be a part of the documents that you will sign at closing, that you will not incur any further liability without their knowledge. They will certainly not accept any existing encumbrances on the pledged property and would want such liens cleared before accepting it as collateral.

Your customer and vendor list: The bank may request that you provide some additional information, like your customer and vendor list and a lot of similar information. All this information will then become part of the decision-making process about the approval of your loan request. This is the lenders' way of making themselves comfortable with the overall business operation and its legitimacy and strength, which will support the amount of loan that they are considering approving for you.

The above list is by no means a comprehensive one. Depending upon your industry and the bank's comfort to extend loans to such an industry, there may be some additions or subtractions to the list of information above. However, let us understand the fact that the banks will want as much information about you and your business as possible to enable them to accept your request for the loan.

Summary of Chapter 14

<u>Secret of Successful Approval of Your Loan</u>

- Information ... Information .. Information

- Explicit Business plan

- Financial Statements

- IRS Returns for Seasoned Businesses

- Cash Flow projections

- Collateral and its Appraisal

- Environment Report

- Receivable Analysis

- Customer and Vendor List

Good packaging of all of the above information.

Chapter 15

How Much is Your Collateral Worth to Lenders?

Collateral plays an important role in reassuring the lenders that in case of default in payment of their money there are enough assets around under their control to be able to make good the shortfall in the loan repayment, through their liquidation. It will be interesting information for the entrepreneur to understand how the lending institutions appraise and value the collateral that you have offered.

The value of anything may be different from different perspectives: With regard to valuation of collateral, the borrower wonders why the lender does not value the collateral that the borrower is providing at its real value. The difference in the market value of the asset and the value accepted by the lender may be large. This may be so large at times that it becomes an issue of contention between the borrower and the lender. However, the reason for this differential is based on certain facts. As in any other issue, if the borrower perceives this issue also from the perspective of the lender and tries to understand the facts behind it, the whole matter may be readily understood. We shall try and reason it out in following paragraphs.

Banks are in business of lending money, not in business of acquiring collateral: The borrower must recognize the fact that the lender is not in the business of selling your assets to satisfy your debts. They are in business of "renting" money and earning a modest additional value in the shape of interest, without going into a hassle of having to liquidate anyone's assets. The lender is also always mindful of the fact that since they are not experts in liquidating assets, they will probably recover a lesser amount of money than what the owner may be able to realize if he himself would liquidate the same. Hence, to be on the safe side, the lender assigns only a discounted percentage of the real market value to the collateral offered. This is to ensure that in the event of the lender having to liquidate those assets, and if the value realized by the lender is lower than the market price, that reduced value may still satisfy the value of loan owed.

On some occasions, the collateral's value accepted by the bank may vary in a wide range of percentage of its appraised or perceived value. The final value may depend on many other factors than a rule of thumb. Here are some of the examples and ranges for guideline purposes only where the lending bank may be ready to accept the value of any collateral while considering a loan.

Cash deposit certificates (CDs): These are taken at 100% of their value, since they have real-money value at the point in time against which a loan is being created.

Stocks and bonds: The value of stocks and bonds keeps changing with the market, economy, and other relevant factors. Hence, to allow for any reduction of value of the stocks and bonds, the lender will allow about 60% to 80% of its value in collateral, depending on the market and quality of stocks.

Receivables: While accepting the receivables as collateral, its aging analysis is a very important factor. If the receivables are current, they may be easily collected without any bad debt. However, if they are older than the normal industry practice, a part of it may not be recovered and may have to be written off as bad debt. The aging of receivables in any business keeps on increasing or decreasing at different times. There are numerous reasons for this fluctuation. Sometimes the manager of the business may not keep a good watch on the receivable and it may increase, and sometimes they increase substantially in a seasonal business. If the lenders were to collect the receivables, it would not be as easy for them to collect all the receivables that the business owner or manager would be able to, because of their personal relationship with the customer. Hence, to allow for some bad debts in the receivables, the lender will accept about 60% to 75% of the total current receivables to be considered against the loan that is being created.

Inventory: When the inventory is pledged as collateral, it is usually a tricky issue for the lender. The inventory is in the possession of the borrower and, hence, theoretically, it may be removed by him without the knowledge of the lender. This is particularly true if the inventory is small in quantity and is highly valuable, like gold or jewelry. Even in case of bulky inventory, the lenders always feel they do not have enough control and, hence, they will allow only 40% to 70% depending on their comfort level with the customer.

By the same token, if the inventory is hypothecated, which means it remains under the custody and lock and key of the lender, only a smaller percentage discount is usually considered. However, this is only possible if the pledged inventory is surplus to normally required levels with the borrower, to allow him to continue his business by selling the inventory in his own possession.

Real estate: Real estate is one of the very standard types of collateral for the lender to accept against a loan. However, the prices of real estate also keep fluctuating. Hence they will allow about 60% to 80% of the appraised value of the real estate for the collateral. They would also like to see that the property being collateralized is clean environmentally and, hence, they will want to have a report on that.

House: In some of states in the U.S. there is a homestead rule, and the lender will not accept the personal residence of the borrower as collateral, since they cannot take it if the loan does not perform. However, loans against the equity in the home may be created under some circumstances.

Now, you, as a borrower, can understand from the perspective of your lender about the worth of your collateral. You should be able to judge as to whether or not your collateral is sufficient to support the requested loan. This exercise of appraisal and evaluation of collateral is a part of the screening by the bank's underwriting department, who work on your loan behind the scenes until it is approved or declined.

Chapter 16

You Have a Commitment Letter—Now What?

Time for negotiation: OK, let us assume that your loan officer tells you that your loan has been approved in principle and that the lender has issued a commitment letter to you mentioning their terms. Congratulations! Now that the bank has, in principle, told you that they are likely to extend a loan to you, this is the time for you to discuss, understand, and, if necessary, negotiate with your bank all the terms and conditions.

Commitment letter: This is usually a two to three page note outlining the basic terms and conditions, acceptable to the lender to create a loan for you. It spells out the amount of loan that you will get, the interest rate, and the term (time period or number of years) of the loan. The letter will also spell out what collateral the lender wants to see and its value.

Understand the terms and conditions: You must ensure that the loan is a good deal for you and your business and fulfills your funding needs. Hence, you need to study and understand the commitment letter thoroughly and discuss all the aspects of it with your lender. You will want to ensure that these terms and conditions are at least fair. From the lender's point of view, they will want to see that their loan is paid back with interest as per agreed terms. They would also assess the risk that they are taking in lending you the money.

Ordering of appraisal and other reports: The next step for the bank would be to obtain professional third-party appraisal and environmental cleanliness on the offered collateral. These reports are ordered to process your loan and are usually at your expense. The lender will want you to deposit the expense amount with them before the reports are ordered.

Analysis of and understanding the commitment letter: Before you give a go-ahead signal to the lender to start spending a lot of time and money, you need a full understanding of the deal you are getting. To further understand this, we shall discuss different parts of the commitment letter and analyze them. This will help the readers and the entrepreneur as to what are "fair terms" while getting a loan. It may be a bit too late to start negotiating these matters when a lot of your money has been spent and a long time has been invested.

Usually, the lender's terms in the commitment letter are fairly standard. Although they may not be negotiable to a large extent, it is important for you to understand all the issues and terms, so as for you to conclude that the terms are fair.

Discussion with the banker: Every condition in the commitment letter will usually have a reason to be there. To understand this, you will need to put your lender's cap on and think from his perspective. This may all be very confusing for a new borrower, though. He may already be so intimidated by the banker and would usually hesitate to negotiate. However, it is usually a good thing to discuss the terms and conditions with the banker. Lenders do not get offended with these discussions at all. In fact, it is their job. Such discussion is in their own interest also. They will then be reassured that you understand the offer fully. At the conclusion of your meeting there may not be any substantial changes in the terms, but such a discussion will usually tell the banker that you are prudent, and he is likely to have better confidence in you.

Your obligations at this stage: The lender will want you to agree to pay the cost of appraisals, environmental reports, and maybe some other costs to start processing your loan request. One word of caution here: if, after all this expense, it is determined that your loan application cannot be approved, your expense is nonrefundable. This process may take typically anything from four to eight weeks depending upon how quickly they find organizations to do these reports. If the report then suggests some doubts, further inspections or inquiries may have to be made. Consequently, it may take longer still, which may be as long as more than three months.

Evaluation of commitment letter and discussion with lender: There are several indicators in the commitment letter of the bank that will tell you if you have a good deal from your bank or not. Conversely, it also reflects how the bank views your credit rating and their risk of the loan. If the bank finds the loan to be riskier than usual because of any reason, its cost will go higher to cover such risk. If the bank finds it very risky, your application will be declined anyway. This may be reflected in one or more of the following indicators. We shall also discuss these factors individually, since each of them have a specific reason to be a part of the commitment letter. Some of these factors are interrelated, and we shall try to analyze and understand them one by one.

Interest Rate: High or reasonable? Interest is the rent that the bank is charging you to let you use the money. This may be high, particularly if they think you are a higher risk for them for any reason. This is almost the same as renting an apartment; if you have children or pets, the rent may be higher, since there is a fear that the property may be abused and, hence, may depreciate faster. Similarly, if the lender thinks that his money is at higher risk, he will increase the interest on it, thereby getting higher reimbursement for taking a larger risk.

In the case of a loan, if your credit is weak but on balance, it is not as bad for the banker to outright refuse you the loan; you are a higher risk. It is very common for the bank to ask for a higher interest rate in such cases, if they think you are a higher risk. This conclusion may be the outcome of any one or a collection of these reasons:

- You may have less than an acceptable range of credit score.

- You may have lack of experience.

- Your business is unusual or exotic, in which the bank has less experience or confidence.

- Your down payment is not enough, as expected by the bank.

- Your business plan may be poorly presented.

- Your guaranty or collateral is not quite up to the mark.

On different kinds of loans the interest rate is different, since the risk taken by the lender to create that loan is considered to be different. However, for a conventional loan, an interest rate of prime plus 2% is generally acceptable, though some customers with a longer banking relationship and better credit rating will get much better terms with a lower interest rate.

Points charged for the approval or availability of the loan: This is yet another tool the banks use to add to their profits. This is viewed as the fees that the bank will charge to make money available to the borrower. However, in practice, the money is already there, and sometimes an abundance of it is available, if the bank's loan-to-deposit ratio is low. Lenders may, in fact, be literally soliciting for the borrowers and paying some finder's fees to someone who brings to them an acceptable borrower to whom they may lend their money with safety. It would certainly be easier for the borrower. Almost all the lenders usually charge one point on the amount of the loan. If it is more than that, there may be some reason, and usually it is negotiable or at least discussed.

"Floor" of the interest rate: This concept ensures the banks earn a larger profit from the windfall of unforeseen low prime rates. The prime rate is the interest rate charged by banks from their most creditworthy customers. These rates are usually fixed on the basis of the lending interest rates fixed by the Federal Reserve. Some banks have started using a concept of floor or lowest interest rate on the loan that they extend. Basically, this is the same as a floating interest rate with an additional condition. For example, the floating interest rate would stipulate, say, prime plus 2%, but not less than 7% floor rate. This means if prime is 6%, then the rate that the borrower pays is $6 + 2 = 8\%$, and if prime is 5%, then $5 + 2 = 7\%$. However, if the prime falls down to 2%, in usual floating rate conditions, the borrower would pay $2 + 2 = 4\%$, but with this condition of a minimum floor interest rate of 7%, the borrower will have to pay the least mentioned "floor" rate, which is the minimum agreed for that loan, even though prime has fallen lower. The minimum floor gives the banks a guaranty of some additional profit if the prime rate falls very low.

Floating rate: Let us recognize and understand that all these institutions are professionally managed. They have an annual projection of earnings and expenses with projected profits. There are goals and targets to be achieved. There is always accountability for almost every action, particularly if the targets are not met, or sometimes even if they are surpassed beyond an acceptable variant, because then it will be seen as having not enough farsighted projections by the responsible managers. Hence, these organizations would like to produce results consistent with their forecast and projections.

Floating rate means a stipulation by the bank that the interest will be prime + X% and will keep on changing if the prime moves higher or lower. The floating rates are preferred by the banks since they will have an almost correct projected profit, since the interest rate may keep on changing as per the need of the economy. However, even with such changes, the banks earn a consistent profit. By studying the trends of the economy, bankers may be able to make an estimate as to whether the interest rates are likely to rise, fall, or stay stable. But bankers are conservative by training and are not in the habit of taking any risks or speculating. Hence, a floating rate is their hedging against a variable prime rate, where they can still keep on charging the same spread.

Banking is a business. They "find" money through CDs at a lower rate of interest, or "rent," and lend it at a higher rate. There are occasions in a moving economy when the Federal Reserve lowers the prime rates substantially. When this happens, the interest rate that the banks are charging the borrower goes down as well, since it is linked with the prime. At that time, the loans that the banks are making are also at a lower interest rate. If the banks have many CDs from customers promising higher rates for a longer period of time, they are likely to lose profit or make lesser profit than the forecast. This is because the sources of their capital are more expensive than the loan interest rate on new loans or in some old loans with fixed interest rate conditions.

Floating rates are preferred by the banks to ensure that if the prime moves higher they may charge more interest on the loan and that they do not have to be bound by the initial lower rates of interest that have been offered. This is again particularly true when the bank forecasters say that the chance of the Prime rate moving higher is larger. This is specifically done when the bank thinks that in prevailing economic environment the interest rates are too low. They project the rates to soon go high and, hence, if they commit themselves for a longer period at a lesser rate, they may lose on that loan

Fixed interest rate: Some banks allow the fixing of the rate by charging some extra interest. While fixing the interest rate, which they do not like, they almost use something similar to actuaries' tables, forecasting what the chances are of interest rates going higher. Hence, to allow the fixing of the interest rates, the bank would ask for some premium over the current rates, which may be anything from 1% to 4% depending upon the forecast about the interest rates, whether it is going to move higher or lower. However, even at that premium the bank may not be very inclined to fix the interest rates in a turbulent economy with a lot of uncertainties. After agreeing to fix the interest rate, they will usually hedge against any loss over the long-period loan, by fixing their rate in the money market over the long term of a loan, ensuring their profit.

Fixed rates are better from the borrower's point of view. This allows the borrower to predict their debt servicing and monthly outgoing for a longer period of time and maintain their profitability. Such a situation will allow them to rest assured over the unpredictability of the rates going suddenly higher, making it difficult to service their debt.

Balloon payment terms: Every businessman would like to pay all his attention to growing his business, rather than worrying about the dates of certain commitments that they have agreed to for the loan borrowings. If these commitments are about providing an inventory or receivables report every month, it may be tailored into normal report preparation and complied with easily. However, one of the usual conditions that the banks have been more frequently inserting in their conditions is that the amortization may be over fifteen or twenty years, but there is a "call" or "balloon payment" every five or seven years. This simply means that the banks have a right to renegotiate the loan terms or even ask for the whole payment and refuse the renewal of loans.

Normally, in a good and regularly paid current loan, the call option is not exercised by the lender to ask for full payment of the loan. However, the call or balloon option certainly brings in an uncertain factor for the borrower; wherein, they have to start talking to the lender well in advance to ensure that the bank will renew the loan and make sure the interest rate will be satisfactory. This ballooning condition may sometimes be beneficial to a new borrower, since it gives the borrower a chance to shop around and find better terms for their borrowings, particularly with a good history of performance of five years or so on the loan they have had.

Prepayment penalty: In some conventional as well as SBA loans, the bank would like to insert his condition that if the borrower wants to pay off earlier than its maturity, there will be a penalty to be able to do so. In recent times, a loan ballooning in five years may typically have 5, 4, 3, 2, or 1% penalty. This means that the borrower will have to pay a penalty of anywhere between 5% to 1%, depending on how early the loan is paid off. Many variations of this condition are applied by different banks. The penalty may be only for first two years at flat rate or there may not be any penalty if you sell the business off, since the new owner may get it financed from his own lending source. This provision is inserted by lender in their term sheet, so as to create a stability in their loan portfolio, whereby they can see that they have an amount of money that will remain employed for a certain number of years. If it is paid off earlier, there will be a penalty amount accrued to offset the time for which the same money may remain idle in their hands, which would otherwise be making some interest earning from the borrower.

It is an instrument with the lending institution that they use to protect and streamline their own working. They would like to know that once they have been through a lengthy process of approving your loan, the amount of capital they have "rented out" at a certain interest rate remains productive and does not come back to them unexpectedly when they may not utilize it fully. Hence, they would create, say, hurdles, in your repayment of the loan, particularly through early prepayment penalty. This is no different than a small-business man, who has made a sale of several items and thinks he has made a certain profit. Then suddenly he finds that his customer brings back all the sold items for return and the expected profit evaporates to almost nothing. In other words, the lenders would like to see what they call "yield maintenance" to be consistent on their extended loans and not let it fall. This clause is also called the "defeasance" clause.

Length of time it has taken to finally get commitment and closing: This is a general indicator that shows how easy or difficult your loan process has been. Though it is too generic and there may be many factors, which affect the turnaround period, it surely shows the efficiency and proficiency of both of the lender and the borrower. Sometimes the underwriting department takes longer than usual to finally come up with an approval and commitment. However, even if all the other factors are equal, it is an indication to you that either the bank is not quite conversant with your industry or they have some issues about the project or the credit of borrowers. Hence, they have taken a much longer time to finally satisfy themselves before coming to a conclusion.

Chapter 17

The "Processing" of Your Loan Application

or

The Evaluation of Your Loan Proposal by the Lender's Underwriters

The processing: Many first-time or even seasoned borrowers do not recognize fully what goes on in the "processing" of a loan. In almost all lending institutions, depending upon their workload and size, there is always a force of personnel called underwriters. This may be an integral part of the loan committee in a small organization, and the loan officer himself may be responsible for it. However, in large organizations, this is a full-fledged department called the underwriting department. They are charged with responsibility to collect and check all the information for its correctness. Their objective is to conclude whether the borrower will have adequate internal cash-flow generation to pay back the proposed loan with its interest as per the agreed terms and conditions. They would also determine that in the event of some unforeseen circumstances of default there is adequate collateral to fall back on to satisfy the loan amount.

Underwriters: It is this department of the organization that is usually "invisible" to the loan applicant and yet carries the ultimate weight to decide the fate of your loan application. The underwriters of the institution carry out this whole "process" of evaluation. Their job is to ensure a thorough analysis of your loan application and all the documents that have been submitted. They would have a checklist of the documents that you need to provide. If any required paper is missing they will pursue it with you before finally deciding your loan application's fate. They will have all the minor details also looked upon before the loan is closed and a check is cut in your name.

As mentioned earlier, the underwriters in any organization are almost invisible because in most of the organizations, the borrower almost never meets the underwriters or even may not have heard this term. The underwriters will usually communicate with the borrowers through their loan officers, unless it is a small organization and the work of loan officer overlaps to some extent with the underwriter. It is their ultimate responsibility to ensure that loan being approved is safe and will be repaid with interest within the agreed time period by the borrower through the generation of cash flow and profit from within the business for which it is given.

Underwriter's recommendations: It is the responsibility of the underwriting-department personnel to evaluate the documentation presented in support of the loan application. Their recommendation to approve or deny the loan will generally carry the most weight for the lending organization. Their negative or affirmative recommendation will decide the fate of your loan application in that direction. Sometimes they ask for further supportive documents from the applicant through the loan officer. This may cause an unnecessary delay in their decision. Therefore, it would be prudent for you to provide all the available and maximum relevant information to the loan officer in the first place to avoid any delay.

Once the underwriter is satisfied that all is well, they signal the loan officer that they have cleared the application to close the loan and provide the funds to the borrower. Closing is the big day when the borrower gets the money that he/she has been looking for to go ahead with their plans.

Criteria of evaluation: There are a few main factors that they will look upon very stringently. We shall look upon these in greater detail one by one. The purpose of this chapter is to try and familiarize the borrowers as to what the underwriters are looking for in the application. Once the borrower understands the mindset of the people analyzing the loan application and the requirements that they would wish fulfilled by the borrower, it will be simple for the borrower to start fulfilling those needs, even without being asked. This will simplify the whole process for both parties. It will also increase the success rate of the loan applications tremendously and will enable the borrowers to get their desired amount of loans at reasonable terms. It is almost like preparing for an examination and knowing in advance what questions will be asked and thus be prepared for them.

The scrutiny of the application is mostly scientific and accurate. However, it may also take into account some subjective facts and information. Most of the information is objective and results into a number that everyone can understand and be on the same page while evaluating it. However, while deciding the fate of the loan application, all the numbers and information may have different priorities and weightage to bring about an outcome of an application in the shape of an affirmative or a negative answer. We shall see this in the next few paragraphs in some detail. The following discussion will bring you to the core of the decision-making process in the lending institution about every loan.

- **Character of the principals and the company:** These comprise many abstract and physical values. The lender will get the history and background of the principals checked. This will include the history of the business, if it is an existing business, and the behavior of the principals in the day-to-day repayment of their obligations. These include the business obligations and also personal obligations. Public record and searches on the past of the principals may be a part of the scrutiny.

  This aspect of analysis comprises of two elements, of which one is tangible and the other is intangible or abstract. The loan officer, usually working as a field officer, will collect information about the business and the reputation of the principals. The underwriters will assess the overall strength of the loan application on the basis of the numbers and formulas, as we shall see in the following paragraphs.

- **Ability of company to repay the loan from the profits, which is termed as a primary source of repayment:** Expert analysts will analyze cash flow of the company. It must show beyond doubt that the company would be able to repay the loan obligation from the profit of the business itself. At times the business may be losing money at the time of the loan application. However, there may be a great opportunity waiting, with the help of additional capital, to make a consistent profit to repay the loan in future. This may have to be explained in the loan application. The loss may only be apparent and not real since it may be arising from owner's drawing of a hefty salary or pension plan, and, hence, the business may be reverted to profit immediately by reconstructing the commitments.

Financial analysis: By far, this is the most important work of the underwriters. The results of this exercise will decide in favor or against the approval of a loan request. To be able to ascertain the ability of the company to repay the loan obligations, the analysts will derive the following mentioned and many other important indicators from the income statement supplied to them. These are all simply mathematical calculations, which is applied to the figures that you have provided. The following information will enable the borrower to know how your application will be analyzed. Once you know this "secret," you may first analyze your application yourself and be certain that all the indicators are within acceptable range of your industry standards. If you find them all to be acceptable, the underwriter will find the same, since it is only simple mathematical calculations.

The indicators, generally called ratios or percentages, that the underwriters and loan officers use are many, and are arrived at by analyzing your financial reports. Some of the usual ones that you should also track on regular basis in your business for periodical evaluation of your performance are mentioned below.

Gross margin percentage: This is a percentage relationship equation between gross profit and total revenue. You may arrive at this figure by calculating

Gross profit

--------------- X 100 = Gross margin %

Total sales

Operating margin percentage: This is the percentage relationship equation between operating profit and total sales. While considering operating profit, you will include depreciation and financial expenses to calculate the percentage of profit over total sales.

Net margin percentage: This is the percentage relationship equation between net profit and total sales. You may arrive at this figure by calculating

Net profit

--------------- X 100 = Net margin %

Total sales

Earnings Before Interest, Taxes, Depreciation, and Amortization (EBITDA): The next thing that the underwriter will want to ascertain is the EBITDA of your business. This is Earnings Before Interest, Taxes, Depreciation, and Amortization. You need to add back to the net profit, the taxes paid, depreciation claimed, and the financial outlay expenses, including interest. Obviously, the EBITDA will be higher than the net-profit figures. However, this is used to calculate the "debt service ratio" or "coverage ratio."

Debt service ratio or coverage ratio: This is an important indicator for the lender to ascertain whether your business will sustain the repayment of the loan with interest at the agreed terms. This is an important relationship between the EBITDA and the amount of repayment of principal plus interest. The amortization tables determine the repayment amount by inserting appropriate numbers for rate of interest, term of loan, and the amount of loan. To arrive at this ratio you need to divide EBITDA by the amount of repayment of principal plus interest (also called debt service). This may be represented as follows:

EBITDA
----------- = Debt service ratio
Debt service

The higher this number, the better it is. This will mean your EBITDA is large enough to comfortably pay the debt as required by the lender.

The underwriter would usually like to see this indicator at 1.3 or higher. This simply means that the lender would like to see you earn at least $1.30, if your debt payment is $1.00, so that you may also be able to pay your other obligations. This ratio indicates to the underwriter how much loan repayment per month or per year the business cash flow and profit will be able to sustain. This is also for the safety of the borrower and ensures for him to remain in business without any default, either towards the bank repayment or any other bills. If this is within their acceptable range, and if other findings are alright, the reply to your application will be in the affirmative; if not, the loan will not be approved. If this indicator is 1.2 or lower, the decision will almost certainly be negative; however, if it is more than 1.4, with other factors being acceptable, the decision will be usually a strong positive for the loan.

- **Credit history of the principals of business:** One of the first things that the underwriters would do is to pull the credit rating of the principals of the business. They will need your permission to do that, which you would have signed off along with the loan application. As mentioned elsewhere in this book, there are three major credit-rating agencies, and the lender may pull the credit record from any or all three of them at their discretion. Again, you may also do this exercise of getting your own credit report before the lender may get at it. This will give you a chance to correct any mistakes in your credit history by communicating with the credit bureaus and rectifying the mistakes. Sometimes the borrower will be surprised to find some bills in collection or some unforeseen situation that may have caused certain lapses in payments. These may then be explained along with the application, or such papers of explanation may be kept ready to supply to the lender when they ask for it.

It is important for the borrower to read the chapter on credit rating and scoring and do their homework to clean up their credit history and score. This exercise will prepare them to be ready for something that they may be expecting through their own homework.

- **Experience of the borrowers in the industry:** This is an important factor that will decide in making or breaking the loan application. One may have a superb location, the right business plan, and financing already available. However, if the principals are not well experienced in the line of business that they want to pursue, the lender will be hesitant to lend the capital, because of unknown risks involved due to inexperience of the principals. They may not be as in control of the business as an experienced businessman would normally be, or they may not be able to withstand some unforeseen situation and, hence, may go into cash-flow problem, or even losses. Therefore, a resume of the principal with details of business experience is an important inclusion in the loan application.

It is easy to understand the value of experience by equating it with the amount of money you are ready to invest in your business as a percentage of the total project amount. This amount is a tangible number, and it is your asset that you are ready to risk for the dream project that you wish to be financed. Experience is also an asset. The only difference being that it is intangible and abstract. Some people do not comprehend how valuable and precious this asset is. However, the fact is that this is an invaluable asset that you possess, and it neither depreciates or gets lost or reduced through use. In the contrary, experience increases and strengthens every day. One may even go to the extent of saying that you may sometimes be able to save your capital investment and that of the lender only if you are appropriately experienced in that line of business.

That's why the lenders take the experience asset of the borrower very seriously to justify and approve the loan application.

- **Collateral offered to ascertain if there is a secondary source for satisfying the loan obligations:** Collateral is not a real reassurance for the lender, since they are not in business of liquidating the assets to satisfy the loan obligations. However, it gives them an idea that if the loan that looks good on day one and goes bad for some unforeseen reason, the lender has enough assets pledged in support of the loan application to fall back on. It also tells the banker, if the business does not perform well, whether or not they will have an ability to loan a further amount to overcome some temporary downturn and, hence, save their own loan amount and the borrower's employed capital from being lost.

- **The principal's investment in terms of percentage of the total project value:** In everyday lingo, this is termed as down payment. In actual fact, the lender wants to see that the principal is contributing reasonably enough capital in the business, showing that he/she is serious on the project, and if need be, is ready to lose his/her savings. This means to the lender that the borrower is not only serious but is ready to show his seriousness by putting a fair sum of money in the business, showing his own confidence and commitment to the business.

A reasonable contribution by the principal in equity of the business will be around 25%. More than 30% would be usually very satisfying to the lender, while anything less than 10% of the project from the principal will almost certainly not be acceptable as a reasonably good down payment for the lender to say yes to the loan.

- **Analysis of income statement and balance sheet of business to ascertain if there is enough working capital with the company:** A working capital need also is calculated from your balance sheet. This is ascertained by looking at how much of the company's money is tied up in receivables and inventory. The less the amount stuck in the receivables and inventory, the less likely is the company to run into any unforeseen cash-flow problem. This is expressed in terms of how many days' sale is stuck in the aging receivables and inventory. And this is calculated very simply by dividing the receivables and inventory figures by the daily sale. One good thing that may transpire from this exercise is that, if the loan is strong from all other angles but does not have enough working capital, the lender may be ready to add the amount they think you might require to the loan. Remember that they want you to be successful to ensure that you do not run into difficulties and, hence, are able to repay their loan as promised. At the end of the day they are looking for a good prospect to loan their money to, so that the unused and excess liquidity that they have may be put to use at an appropriate interest earning.

Approval of loan: A commitment letter is a tentative approval of your loan request. It is subject to confirmation of the values of collateral, environmental cleanliness, finding some acceptable ratios and percentages by analyzing your financials, and checking many other factors. This is all included in the processing of the loan application by the underwriters. When all that is checked and found satisfactory, the bank is ready to part with money. This means that after you had been issued the commitment letter, the bank's underwriters or the loan committee has found that requirements like the appraisals and other reports are good enough for them to agree to accept and fund your loan application. The approval is the final, end result of the evaluation. Once the underwriter gives a go-ahead signal to approve and fund the loan, it then leads you to the closing of the loan.

Section Three

Some Applied Common Sense for All Entrepreneurs

Chapter 18

How Creditworthy Are You in Your Lender's Eyes?

Your creditworthiness is the most important factor that will decide the fate of your loan application. If while evaluating all the information, the lender thinks that you are creditworthy, and that their loan will be repaid without difficulty, your loan will be approved. If not, it will be declined.

The creditworthiness is part of a composite picture: This composite picture has two distinct parts. One is objective and the other is subjective. Both of these parts will paint a picture to lead the banker to decide whether you and your business are worthy of extending a loan that you have requested.

Objective factors making up your creditworthiness: We have already mentioned in this book at length in different places the objective factors that are taken into account to ascertain your creditworthiness. We shall enumerate some of these important factors here, which may be measured numerically.

- **Your credit score:** This is perhaps the most important factor today in lending and in the financial world about one's creditworthiness. This provides the best objective assessment of the credit history that you may have created for yourself. This has become the single most important tool in almost all the lending institutions. This tool is also used by many other credit-giving agencies or those looking at one's trait and trend of being trustworthy or creditworthy. You may come across the credit-score checking while renting an apartment or an office or wishing to be a customer of any business where a credit is extended. They would want to see what your credit history has been plus your payment capability.

  Use of credit score has become such a prevalent and important part of everyone's life that we have devoted one

whole chapter to explain how to keep a track of it. (See chapter 23) Three major credit bureaus keep track of most of the credit transactions taking place almost everywhere. Even before looking at other important pros and cons of whether to lend to you or not, the lender "pulls up" your credit report to see whether it will be worth their while to spend time in going any further in considering you as one of their borrowers.

- **Your business plan, cash flow, and profitability projections:** All these serve as important supportive factors for the lender to deduce whether the loan that they are considering may be approved or declined. Consequently, these become the other important objective elements of your overall creditworthiness.

- **Your down payment and equity participation:** This is yet another factor that allows the lender to assess your commitment into the business that you are proposing.

- **Report about your business from reporting agencies:** There are certain agencies that have specialized in reporting on business as a whole. The most widely used source for such reports is **Dun & Bradstreet (D&B)** on small or large businesses. Another similar source for company reports is **CAROL**, which is an online service offering direct links to the financial pages of listed companies in Europe and the U.S. Yet another source is **AWARE**, which specializes in competitive and marketing intelligence and is recognized as an expert in this field in English-speaking countries.

- **The underwriter's analysis of your financial reports:** Underwriting is the most important, though behind the scene, analysis of you and your business. The underwriter's assessment may be the final word in the decision about the fate of a loan application.

Some subjective factors making up your creditworthiness: Although many factors are taken into account to decide this, some of the important factors are about you personally. Hence, it is important for you to understand them and, if possible, address them beforehand. Since these abstract factors also play an important role in the final impression about your creditworthiness, it is important for everyone to try and start being sensitive to these early in life. Whatever you do in your life from the late teens in practical life to the time you find yourself in a borrowing situation becomes your resume for a lender. Your maturity and discipline in financial matters will especially become a guideline for the lender to decide about your loan application.

- **While the credit score is objective, the credit history is subjective:** Your credit history in general creates a subjective impression for the lenders. Thus, they may not be able to use it with full force and indiscriminately. Guidelines of the regulators for the banks may not include such subjective methods for fear of being a basis of discrimination while considering a loan request. The lender may even be ready to discuss these subjects with you openly as these elements will certainly bear heavily as part of their overall decision and judgment to accede to your request for a loan.

- **Your networking in the community:** As is said, "One is known by the company he keeps." This is one of the important areas that the banker might depend upon. Your involvement in community and your networking with people, who are movers and shakers and are reputable in community, is an important aspect of your life. This will have a large impact on the thinking of your banker when he/she is to decide about the fate of your loan application. Your networking will be a reference in itself. In fact, through your networking, you may have participated in the same or similar programs of community development that your banker may have been involved in the past. He may, in that case, already know you and would not need any introduction or reference.

- **Your reputation in business and the community:**
Remember that it does not only suffice to be actively involved
in the community; you must also create a good impression
on your colleagues, thereby earning a reputation as team
worker. In fact, everyone knows someone who is involved in
community but has a bad reputation because of his attitude
or some other reason. As a good and useful member of
the society, everyone must endeavor to do positive things
according to the customs and traditions of the society that
one lives in.

- **Your reputation as a paymaster:** Depending upon how old
you are and where you are in your career path, you may have
come across many situations where you were supposed to
make a payment on a certain day and date. It may be simply
a payment of your fees, or a telephone or a utility bill. Or it
may be a repayment of some small sum that you may have
borrowed from your friend, relative, a credit-card company,
your university, or a bank. Information about whether you
have been a good and timely paymaster or not gets generally
known through the grapevine and becomes a part of your
overall picture of creditworthiness.

- **References about you from someone that banker knows
well:** If you are new in town or to the bank, it will be a
good idea to have your introduction made to the banker by
someone you know who also knows the banker. One of the
best introductions will be from your CPA who also knows
your business very well, or your attorney. It is always better
to have someone you know to inform your banker of some
nice, yet accurate, facts about you and your business. If that
reference is coming from your CPA, who may also be in the
know of why and how much capital your business needs, the
whole process may be quite simplified.

- **Facts or news and rumors about your past:** As they say,
the news about your financial health and rumors usually

precede you wherever you go. Hence, in the same context, before you even have an appointment to meet your bankers, information about you may already have been heard or known by them from a third and unrelated party. Hopefully this information is positive and good, or at least neutral. If it is not so good, then perhaps the damage is already done. Bankers shouldering responsibility as trustees are, by nature, conservative and even suspicious. They will tend to listen and accept all the negative reports, and these get stored in their minds. You may be able to negate such an impression only if given a chance, which in practical life may not come by, leaving your banker prejudiced about your virtues. It is important therefore to always create a good credibility and reputation about yourself.

- **Resumes of your team members in your business and your experience:** This may also be termed as a subjective evaluation. This also plays an important part in you being considered as creditworthy.

In conclusion, the fate of your loan request depends upon how the banker thinks you will meet your commitment to repay the loan and, hence, it is your credibility in the eyes of the lender that will be the deciding factor to get your loan request approved.

Chapter 19

How to Turn Your Banker
into a Friend Forever?

Your banker is a trustee of the depositors: Your lender has a fiduciary responsibility. Hence, he has a trusteeship obligation toward his depositors. You, being a customer, are also an important person in his life. It is his business to get the deposits from depositors and then "sell" or "rent" that money. Hence, it is also an important job for him to find good customers who are trustworthy and reliable to loan that money to. He needs good people like you who will return that money with its interest as agreed. However, when push comes to shove, the lender is obliged to be more faithful and loyal to his depositors than to the borrower.

When you are in need . . . I remember someone telling me metaphorically a long time ago that the banker will be ready to lend you an umbrella when it is not raining, and if he has to, he may take it away just when it is raining and you need it. It sounded too cynical to me then that a respectable and responsible person of the community like a banker would be ready to help you when everything looks and sounds normal, but would shy away from doing the same thing when you are showered over with business and financial difficulties. However, with the experience of many decades of dealing with banks, it is perhaps partially true but for some right reasons. Because his primary accountability is to his depositors, your banker friend will think many times before giving you a helping hand at your lean and difficult time. However, it is in such situations that an experienced lender, who has developed a sixth sense to assess his borrowers comes handy. That is why you should try and work with seasoned lenders and create a long term relationship with them, which becomes helpful in such odd circumstances. If he feels confident about you, he may justifiably be ready to assist you even in unusual situations.

Your banker needs you as much: After a long time of having been involved in borrowing and lending as part of loan committees, I realize that the banker is obliged to be prudent. He has to be extremely conservative, and cautious in lending, lest the loan goes bad. His very job depends on his being shrewd to the extent of being ruthless under some circumstances. That's why, the statement about lender taking away umbrella when it is raining, may sound unfair, cruel, or even downright nasty about the lender community. Nevertheless, in practice, they act in a balanced way to ensure that their trusteeship position is not compromised and that their fiduciary responsibility, legally and even morally, remains defensible. Bankers, while needing you as much, put up a stance of being tough with the borrowers because they are primarily looking after the depositor's interests. In practice, though, this is an ongoing game of calculations on the part of lender. Despite his ultraconservative approach, he has to find creditworthy persons to entrust them with the depositor's money in the shape of loans.

The bank's support is directly proportionate to your reliability factor: With such difficult responsibility to shoulder and yet having to find good and reliable customers to whom the money can be loaned to, the lender always remains on the lookout for good, honest, and reliable businesspeople. This is a difficult balance to keep and maintain for anyone. The lender usually does not have the luxury to create a friendship with the borrowers because of the peculiar nature of his job. However, at the end of the day, the lenders are human beings, and they learn every day. They become good mind readers and person readers as they become more and more experienced in their job. They keep their antennas up almost all the time to try and receive any good or not-so-good signals about their borrowers. Eventually, they become so good that they can almost tell within first few minutes of their meeting with a prospective borrower whether the prospect will turn out to be a good customer or not.

Expect a good banking relationship? Be a good and reliable customer: Here we are concerned with the usual daily-life issues of how to create a good relationship with your lender and then how to sustain it over a long period of time. As discussed earlier, the lender may not have a lot of close friends from his customer base because the nature of his work would not allow him a close friendship, since it may create a conflict of interest. However, it is not difficult for the customer like you to gradually win over the confidence of not only your lender but also the whole of his team at the lending institution. This requires that you only understand what the right things are to do and how to interact with the bankers.

In effect, the question that we are trying to discuss and resolve is, "How do you enjoy a good relationship with your banker?"

Make the banker look good to the regulators, and he will be your friend: In short, it may be said in general that your banker will be your best friend provided your dealings with the bank remain within the required parameters. The lender must feel that you are a good customer who complies with all the requirements, because, in turn, they have to comply with the regulators. Amongst themselves, they sometimes call it "babysitting" the loan. If the loan performs well, they look good to their superiors, and if it does not, they will be taking the heat. That's why if you make them look good to their higher-ups, they are your friends. Not only this is easy, but it is mandatory as part of the performance of your loan repayment and fulfillment of its conditions.

Regular and timely installment payments: They will soon know that you are paying you installments regularly as per the term sheet. This is by far the most important element of the relationship. The lender will also find out if your business is performing as per projections that you submitted with loan application, from the monthly or quarterly financial reports that you will submit. In any lending institution, you will deal with two or three people, and they will be responsible for making sure that the loan performs well.

Submit fully to the demands of regulators: The parameters that the lender wishes you to observe diligently are to ensure that they, in turn, may be able to comply with the demands of the regulators. These parameters are your contractual obligations to fulfill as part of the terms and conditions of the loan. If you fulfill them with a smile it is good. If you don't, you will be made to do that anyway, if you want a long-term relationship. Hence, why not to submit fully to the demands of the regulators? These requirements are usually not impossible or even difficult. If you observe proper discipline, it is perhaps the easiest thing to do. In fact, by complying with these requirements, you may be doing a lot of good to yourself and your business, since information in all of this reporting will give you a lot of insight into how your own business is doing and progressing. We shall discuss some of the important aspects of this here.

Be your own inspector and auditor: One of the best principles to understand the expectation of others is to try and put yourself in their shoes You must educate yourself to imagine yourself in your banker's shoes and think of the loan performance from his perspective. This is the best advice that you may get as a borrower. To understand the lender's requirements, you will need to do some reading and self-education. It does not mean you need to go back to school, but certainly you need to follow a necessary drill. Its advantages will be tremendous. You may have started your dream business, and you may be getting rich through it. However, if you cannot or do not nurture the banking relationship with care, your dream business may turn into a nightmare.

Keep your promises: Hence, in simple terms, try and understand what your lender expects from you. In the following paragraphs, we have tried to identify the needs of the lender after providing a loan. If his needs are fulfilled, as per your promise, you are likely to get the best-customer award and be the ideal blue-eyed company for the lender. This is all because they have to be answerable to their auditors and regulators. If you are regular in providing them regular updates of the sales, profits, income statement, receivables, and other reports as promised by you while signing the promissory note, the lender will have no ax to grind with you, since their auditors will not hassle them. However, if all those requirements are not fulfilled within due dates, and, hence, if their feathers are ruffled by their regulators, there will be no one more sore and red-eyed than your bankers. They might even wake up you up in morning and ask you to provide whatever is missing to save their skin and your loan from getting classified, which is any lender's nightmare.

So, in order to be a good borrower, you need to equip yourself with some information. They are all out there in the documents that you have signed while closing the loan. All commercial loans will have at least three important documents:

Promissory note

Security agreement between you and the bank

Personal guarantees

Be conversant with the contents of the promissory note: To be able to do this, you need to read through the promissory note at least once that you have signed and given to the bank. This contains a lot of legal jargon, but its reading will tell you what you have promised, on the basis of which you have procured the loan. Apart from your regular payment, these promises are about furnishing some reports at periodic intervals. Its compliance, in turn, ensures that the loan remains current and in good shape.

The promissory note contains important information about:

your interest rate

the term of the loan

the amortization period and schedule

ballooning in the interim period.

Important things that you might want to look at in the promissory note are the provisions of curing the default if it occurs and the rights of setting off other assets against this loan. If you have questions, you need to speak to the bank officers, and if you have any worries about the language in the document, it will be prudent to speak to your attorney before signing it.

Know your loan's terms and conditions: There are some routine things in the loan documents, copies of which will be given to you at the closing of the loan. These consist of many regulatory forms that the bank is obliged to give you as disclaimers or waivers to ensure that it remains in compliance with the regulations. These consist of declarations like equal-opportunity lenders, no other verbal agreement other than the documents signed, and so forth.

Security agreement between you and the bank: This enumerates the collateral that you have provided to the bank, over which they create a security agreement, which is filed with the county clerk. This will also spell out your obligation to keep the collateralized assets in good shape, duly insured, and to keep the lender informed of any material change. It is through this document that the bank takes control of the collateral, if needed, through a legal process called foreclosure.

When the bank provides you a loan, it would want to be the first in line of lien through their security agreement. If you are buying on credit from your vendors and have agreed to give them a security interest, the vendors would generally accept to be after the bank in lien registration. They also recognize that bank has a higher stake in your business.

Personal guarantees provided by you: Banks would like to see that their money is secured in more ways than one. For this reason they will try and get a lot of collateral, and on top of it, they will want your personal guaranty to support the lending. The purpose behind all this is that in some unforeseen situation, if the business cannot repay the loan, the bank will first look at the collateral and try making good on the loan amount. However, the collateral may consist of inventory, machinery, real estate, and personal guarantees backed by financials of the guarantors.

You may remember from what has been mentioned earlier that the banks are in the business of "renting" money only. They are not in the business of acquiring properties and selling them or selling someone's inventory to recover their loan amount. Hence, in case of default in a nonperforming loan, the lender will look at the easiest way of making good on their loaned amount, which in their eyes would be cash money from the guarantor instead of having to liquidate other collateral. If the principal supporter of the business, who has cosigned the loan with a guaranty, has enough money, the pressure will be on them to make up the outstanding balance of the loan with cash. This will save the bank from doing something that they are not good at, which is trying to liquidate inventories, machinery, or real estate. Instead, the bank will get the cash reimbursed from the guarantor.

Subordination agreement: The banks would want as big a protection for the recovery of their loan as possible. Hence, they will want you to sign an agreement of subordination of all the assets of the company and business along with the security agreement. This will mean that any assets already present and created in future, like the receivables generated from the selling of products or services by the business, will stand under the first or prior lien of the lender. Hence, in an eventuality of default, the bank will have a first right to receive it. In other words, if there is another creditor who also has a lien on the assets of the company, your lending institution would want a subordination agreement of their lien to be first, or senior, and that of any other creditor to be second, or junior. The bank may then stipulate to have a formal three-party agreement wherein the outside creditor will accept the priority of lien of the bank and they themselves will shift next to them lower in the lien precedence line. This agreement will have to be made according to the instructions from the legal department of the bank.

Landlord's consent: When the business is operating from leased premises, then the loan proceeds are being invested in a third party's asset and property, which is the landlord. The landlord may have better control of the destiny of the business through the lease condition, which provides him certain lien rights against the assets of the tenant. Hence, before the bank parts its money to be invested in the leasehold premises, it will want what is called a Landlord's Consent. This, in effect, is a subordination agreement of the liens held by the landlord, which lets their position in the lien list be below the bank's position. This consent may also provide a disclaimer of interest by the landlord for most of his interest in the assets of the business, except ownership of the leased premises. It may also ask to add a permission to enter the leased premises by the bank's nominated persons to recover the assets.

Covenants in the loan approval: There are some other provisions that you may see in the documents that the bank will want you to sign. One of the important ones in the eyes of the bank is that you will not incur any further debt without letting them know first, and that they may refuse to let you do that. This is again primarily for the protection of the loaned amount, which becomes compromised if there is a larger debt burden on the business, because of which it might fail.

Yet another condition from the lender may be that they may not allow any further liens even after their senior position, and they may have to be asked and taken permission from, to be able to that. This is to protect the company and business from a very large debt, which may force the business into bankruptcy if the debt repayment is not satisfied, jeopardizing the whole business along with all the investments and liabilities.

Bankers do not like surprises: Bankers are generally very conservative and would like to see things happening as per plan. Anything out of the ordinary does not bode well with them. They also would like to know things in advance if there is going to be anything different happening than what has been planned or projected. Hence, if you think you are likely to be late in payment or may need some more money for your working capital or cash flow, or some other facility, try and inform them in advance, so that they are prepared for it. Do not spring surprises on them, or they will lose confidence in you. Even a small matter of not being able to cover an issued check with an appropriate deposit must be informed to your loan officer well in advance. You must not wait for him to phone you to inform you about the shortfall in your account and having to create an overdraft for you.

In short, open communication and continuous dialogue with your bank about anything new or changes in your business always helps. Such information flow will increase the mutual confidence and, hence, promote a better relationship.

Learn how the bank and their regulators view you as a customer: This is the public-relation aspect of your business. By regularly meeting your banker and discussing the overall situation about your loan and other business conditions, you may remain in continuous know of the views of your banker about you and your business, and, hence, your loan. Every so often the banks are audited by different regulatory agencies, who keep on evaluating the loan portfolio of the bank. Your loan may be one of the loans that they have looked upon and may have commented on or just examined. If there has not been any comment, it is good. If they comment, criticize, or observe upon any part of the loan, it is considered adverse or negative by the bankers. The banker will tell you if there is anything that you need to do to help them to keep those comments away.

Chapter 20
Fulfill Your Obligations and Make Your Lender Your Friend

In previous chapters we have tried to analyze and suggest how to have the best relationship with your banker. However, the secret of having the best of relationship with your lender for the longest possible time is in understanding of your obligation as a borrower to the lending institution. If this is understood well and followed up with diligently, you will automatically have a congenial relationship with your lender without even having to make any additional effort. If you understand your obligations and try and fulfill them without any lapse, you will be the darling of the lending institution, wherever you may be.

There are many conditions that are spelled out in your promissory note, which needs to be understood and kept a note of. However, your obligations as a "good" borrower are simple, logical, and commonsensical. If you follow this broad guideline, which has been repeated often, to look at your obligations from the lender's point of perspective, you will always be doing just the right things. You will never feel that the lender is at your back wanting you to do some useless piece of reporting.

Timely payments: The first and foremost of a borrower's obligations is to pay the loan installments within the guidelines of the terms of the promissory note. That means paying the required amounts at the given date and not even a day late. There are certain grace-period concessions in the note, but try to avoid using those facilities. The best way is to get the lender to draw from your account automatically through electronic methods now usually employed by almost all the institutions. This will throw out all those possibilities of you or your colleague forgetting, holidays falling on the date of payment, or paying late due to any unforeseen reasons.

Since this is first and foremost and most visible proof of your fulfilling your repayment obligation, it cannot be overstressed to observe it most diligently. Any delays and indiscipline will be recorded and will be used against you in your credit history. Hence, you must try and use the new systems of automatic bank drafting, which will almost never let you be tardy in your repayment of installments. Using the bank's auto-debit system will help you avoid any unintentional delays and set you free of any such worries, because it will take the necessary amount from your designated account on the due date.

Regular reporting: In almost every loan there is always some reporting requirement. This may be quarterly, monthly, or even more frequent, depending upon the nature of business.

- **Financial reports:** The lender will certainly want to see a periodical financial report of the business for which they have loaned you the money. It may be more often, but usually a quarterly report containing profit and loss and balance sheet generally suffice. The lender would like to keep track of your performance against the projections that you have supplied at the time of applying for the loan. If there is a gross variance in performance while comparing against the projections, they may want to meet you so you can explain the reasons for such differences. It is usually prudent to insert some notes to explain such variances while submitting these performance reports to preempt their queries and worries.

- **Receivables and aging of receivables report:** Particularly if the receivable is collateral, the lender will also want to keep a close eye on your receivable and may need to have a statement of aging every month. These reports will give them a comfort by ensuring that the receivables are at an agreed level and that the aging is not getting too old. The lender would like to see these receivables high and also current. Your agreed loan is a percentage of "good" receivables and not of doubtful ones.

- **Inventory reports:** Depending upon the nature of your business and if the inventory is collateral, the lender will want you to submit a regular, usually a monthly, report of the inventory that you are carrying. They would like to see that the inventory is held at a comfortable level. This will mean that you are continuing the business as per plan and that their collateral is safely in place. In some cases, you should not be surprised if the banker wants to visit the business premise at regular intervals. One purpose of the visit would be for them to get firsthand visual satisfaction that all is well at the business premises, including the inventory and business activities.

The lender needs some of these reports to keep a watchful eye on your business performance for their own satisfaction. However, these reports are also required by the regulators who want to keep an eye on the banking operations, and they can only do this through your files and the reports provided by you.

Regulators consider regular reporting very important. Therefore, your bank will have some employees assigned to interact with the borrowers and ensure that these reports are received in timely manner and that your file is kept current for the regulators to see. If these reports are missing, the regulators might "observe" or "criticize" such a loan, which is neither good for you or for the bank. On many occasions, not submitting such reports when due, cause an unhappy relationship between you and your banker. You may avoid such issues by adhering to a discipline of regularly sending the promised reports.

Prearrange facility with your bank: One thing that the banker does not like is some unforeseen surprise in the management of your account. One of the common mistakes that a number of new business owners commit is to issue checks when an adequate balance is not there or the checks in hand are not deposited. If issuing a check is a well-thought-out cash-flow exercise after a long enough experience in business, it may be alright. However, in a new business, if you write a payment check in the expectation of some incoming checks that are not in your hands or even on the basis of some checks that you are depositing but are not certain will be honored, you may be in for a surprise. When your check is presented to the bank for payment, there may not be enough balance to cover the amount. This is what bankers dislike the most, and you are immediately in their bad books.

You may be a good customer, but… Do you see what you have done? Your account manager is presented with a difficult choice to bounce your check, since your balance is a few hundred dollars short and you have not intimated your banker beforehand that this might happen. Your bank may have extended you several hundred thousand dollars' worth of a loan, and you may be paying it as a good customer. That's why he may not like to hurt your credit by dishonoring your check, which has been presented without a prearranged overdraft request. However, he may not have an authority to create that overdraft for you, since in different institutions this authority will reside with different positions. When you need it, that person holding a higher position and having such authority may not be available. The most serious matter here is the fact that this is a financial indiscipline, which is not liked by any banker.

Early-morning rude surprise: Hence, you have put your banker in a dilemma by springing an early-morning surprise. He may eventually solve it by finding you on the phone and getting a promise to cover the amount of the check within a few hours and get a temporary overdraft authorized. However, the fact is that you have put a wrench in his normal daily routine. Avoid this as best as you can. If it is totally unavoidable, pick up the telephone and inform your banker that this may happen unexpectedly and was not in your control. Better still, if this is likely to happen more often, visit your banker and explain to him the situation, and he will be amenable to create an overdraft facility to you temporarily. After all, if they have entrusted you with a substantial loan and you have already shown a streak of being a good paymaster, he will not be that worried about extending some more credit.

Create open-channel communication with banker: The biggest pitfalls in the banking relationship that one may think about, is not having open communication with your lender. The example of informing the banker in advance if there is an unexpected presentation of a check when the balance may fall short is the best example of open communication, and the banker will oblige you in most cases. If it comes as a surprise to him, he is bound to be angry and even uncooperative.

Requirements are easy to fulfill: There are no unusual requirements to be fulfilled and, hence, there are no real pitfalls in your repaying or fulfilling the requirements of ensuring a well-performing loan. If you have understood your obligations well, generally there should not be any worry about any strained relationship with your lender.

Ballooning of your loan: In conventional loans, you may have a fifteen- or twenty-year amortization, but there may be a five- or seven-year call of the note. If you have been regular in payment, then the bank will want to renew the loan without any hassle, because it would not want to let a good customer go to some other lender. However, if you have been creating problems for the bank in being a tardy paymaster and not providing the necessary reports in time, it is their chance to ask you to go and find a new lender.

At this ballooning time, the terms of the loans may be renegotiated, or either party may wish to come out of the obligation. This may happen if you find another lender who might give you better terms and conditions, or you may need an amount bigger than your present lender may be willing to extend. On the lender's part, he may have not found you very disciplined and may wish to discontinue the relationship, or the institution is getting out of the business or industry that you are in as a matter of policy.

Renegotiation of terms at call time: Depending upon the economy and financial situation, the bank may also want to raise the interest rate on the loan, or raise the floor of interest rate. If the interest rates are lowering, then it is your chance to ensure that you get the benefit of the lower interest rate, which, if the existing lender is not ready to accept, you may find some other lender who may accommodate your needs. With a five years' history of regular payment and business history, you are likely to get a better deal from some alternative lender.

However, it must be added here that almost all loans, barring only a few, will have such issues coming up in their lifetime. Hence, the ballooning dates only remain a formality to be observed.

Yet, it is your responsibility as a prudent businessperson to remember such dates and put them somewhere on the calendar. You must then try and discuss with your banker a few months in advance whether there is any likelihood of any changes and, hence, prepare yourself so as not to face any surprises at the last moment.

Provide information to the bank within the required time: This is almost a repetition of what has been said in other paragraphs in this chapter. The banks always are insistent on getting the information that you have agreed to provide on a regular basis. It is because the regulators want to have all the reports on file to evaluate the performance of your loan. Even if all the payments are being made on the due date, the report submission is still important from the regulator's and banker's point of view. Without such reporting, your loan file is considered to be incomplete and, hence, the regulators and auditors may harass your lender for that. If this happens on a regular basis, the banker would also create a dislike for your account.

Lean time for business? Learn to tide over the difficulties in cash flow because of unexpected situations. Some businesses are seasonal, and they have a known lean period when you may need the bank's help in cash flow or working capital. In others, the overall economy may take the toll with any downturn, and, hence, may create an unforeseen situation. However, if you are likely to project and foresee such situations coming, it will be prudent for you to inform your lender in good time to ensure it is not a surprise for them. In fact, the lender will be more supportive if he is told the situation in advance. Again, this is also an exercise in good communication, which will help you in having a better understanding with your banker.

Summary of Chapter 20

Your Obligations after getting your loan & How to be a good borrower

- Timely Installment Payments.

- Regular Reporting

  - Financial Reports

  - Receivables reports

  - Inventory Reports

- No surprises for your banker.

- Open and continuous communication.

Section Four

Some Accounting

"Wisdoms"

Chapter 21
Cash Flow and Its Management

Planning in life: Planning is one of the most essential tools that may be used in almost any and every walk of life. You may plan which road to take to avoid traffic and save time. Or you may plan to negotiate a deal in a particular fashion to get the maximum benefit from it. Similarly, in business, planning is a very vital and significant part of the whole process.

Planning in business: All business analysts agree that poor planning and management is the main reason for business failure. Of all the other factors, poor cash management is the most important and frequent failing of a new business. A business consists of many components, like sales, purchasing, advertising, personnel management, banking, and so forth. All these components need to be planned properly to obtain an outcome in the shape of profit for that business. Yet, one more component, which is central to all the others, is the cash flow of the business, and its management is the most important part of the business.

Understanding business cash flow: We need to understand the importance of the positive cash flow in any business and some salient factors that affect it. First of all, let us understand that every business has to have a positive cash flow. The business may afford to run into a negative cash flow only temporarily. However, even that temporary period has to be covered with some arrangement to ensure that your obligations are paid through bridge financing or a personal cash injection so that you do not run into default of your obligations.

Reputation of a business: The reputation of any business, large or small, primarily depends upon how regularly you are meeting your payment obligations. These payments may be salaries, utilities, vendors, supplies, and creditors. Even a slight but recurrent delay or nonpayment are considered as default, which will tarnish the reputation of the business. It may then create a vicious circle of not being supplied with inventory by vendors; hence, you'll have fewer sales, resulting in even the utilities being cut off and business coming to a halt. As you may see, a very bleak picture is drawn here if the cash flow is not kept viable to pay all the bills in time. However, this is the key to any business, and the owners/managers must always remain on top of it.

Planning the cash flow; crystal ball for operator: The tool to plan the cash flow is called the cash-flow projection. This may almost be termed as a crystal ball for the managers of the business, since if prepared and used correctly and frequently, it will help ensure the business runs smoothly. This exercise of cash-flow projection will bring many unforeseen possibilities into light and, hence, allow you to plan for it in good time. It will also give you an opportunity and ability to rectify any problems that may be looming in future and address them before they become a worry for you.

What is cash flow? Cash flow refers to the movement of cash into and out of a business. Watching the cash inflows and outflows is one of the most important and ongoing management tasks for any business. The outflow of cash includes those checks you write each month to pay salaries, utilities, suppliers, expenses, and repayment of debts. The inflow includes the cash you receive from customers' revenue, receivables, lenders, and investors.

Smart business owners would learn how to develop both short-term (e.g., weekly, monthly) cash-flow projections to help them manage daily cash, and long-term (e.g., annual, three- to five-year) cash-flow projections to help them develop the necessary capital strategy to meet their business needs. They also prepare and use historical cash-flow statements to understand how they used money in the past.

Understanding the difference between cash, profits and assets: Cash is ready, and liquid money is in the bank or in the business. Cash is what you must have on hand to keep your business running. Inventory, accounts receivable (what you are owed), machinery, and property are assets. Surely, assets are an important capital of the business. However, although they can potentially be converted to cash sometimes, they cannot be used as ready cash to pay suppliers, rent, or employees' salaries. A large asset and sizeable projected profits do not necessarily mean more cash on hand. Profit is the amount of money you expect to make over a given period of time. Over a long period of time, a company's good projected profits may not help if the receivable remain unpaid, causing the business to run into negative net cash flow. You can't spend profit unless it converts into cash. In such cases again, bridge financing may be helpful to tide over the hump of negative cash flow. However, both these situations (e.g., a spot of negative cash flow and the need of short-term borrowing) would be evident in your cash-flow projection.

Positive cash flow and profitability: Sometimes the beginner in business takes a simplistic view that if he is making profits, he will have a positive cash flow. This is not necessarily true in practice. While making good profits, the business may run into serious negative cash-flow problems if there is a large account of receivables. Conversely, though, while making losses, there may be an apparent and deceiving positive cash flow for a short period of time.

Some bankers are attuned to look very closely at the personal cash flow of the guarantors of the loan, which they expect to be strongly positive. This is a smart way of getting an indirect indication that the loan will be paid back without difficulty from an alternative cash-flow stream even if the business may not be in profit or has a negative cash flow. It also tells the lender that if the owner/guarantor has a positive cash flow, the owner will not use the business cash flow to meet his personal negative cash flow.

Positive Cash Flow: If the cash inflow exceeds the outflow, a company has a positive cash flow. A positive cash flow is most essential and a good sign of financial health in terms of short-term management. However, by itself, it may not necessarily be a definitively positive indicator for the overall health of the business.

Positive cash flow does not mean profits: Positive cash flow does not necessarily mean that the business is making a profit. Even if the business is making a profit, the business may still run into a serious cash-flow problem because cash is not available when needed. This statement may sound far too elementary for a seasoned businessman. Nevertheless, on so many occasions, we have seen that the entrepreneurs or even persons in ongoing businesses do not quite understand the difference between the two. We would like to emphasize this with examples for those who are new in this game to ensure there is a clear understanding of the need to stay on top of the cash-flow situation.

For example: A business is selling a lot of goods and its revenues are very high. However, if its payment terms are such that the cost of goods and raw material is to be paid at a later date and the customers are paying cash for what they buy, as it happens in a retail business, this will evidently result in a positive cash-flow situation, since the revenue is collected and is not due for payment until later. However, if in the same business, the overheads are very high and the cost of production is higher than the sale price, the business is making a loss while showing a deceivingly high positive cash flow.

Negative Cash Flow: Simply put, if the cash outflow in a business exceeds the inflow, a company has a negative cash flow. Reasons for negative cash flow include too much or obsolete inventory and poor collections on accounts receivable (what your customers owe you). If the company can't borrow additional cash at this point, it may be in serious trouble, since it cannot pay off its obligations on time and will become a defaulter.

Negative cash flow does not necessarily mean losses: While conversely looking at the earlier example, let us see what happens if a business is selling its goods at a definitely large net profit. While doing so, if it is supposed to be paying its vendors in short time (since a short credit period has been agreed), while the customers are going to pay at a much later date (given a long credit), the business will run into a serious negative cash flow problem, despite making healthy profit.

Usage of cash-flow projections as a tool: Examples in both the above situations can be handled fairly easily if they are known in advance, which is the function of the cash-flow projections. For the preparation of such projections, there will have to be an intimate understanding of all the elements of the business. Having prepared the projections, the business owner would need to continuously monitor the business activities by proper cost analysis, ensuring a reasonable profit.

It is essential, particularly for the beginners, to anticipate such a situation through such projections. In the first example, the owners may have a false impression of everything being well with positive cash flow, while at the end they will realize that the income statement shows a loss in the bottom line. In the latter example, the negative cash flow will need to be rectified quickly to avoid the unpleasant experience of facing creditors, who, despite having made a healthy profit, cannot be paid over a short run as per the promise, causing a lot of embarrassment. Such a situation may also result in a strained relationship with vendors because of a default in promises to pay and also a tarnishing of the business reputation.

If known in advance through the cash-flow projections, when needed and as indicated by the cash-flow analysis, a short-term loan may be obtained in good time to cover the negative cash flow to circumvent such a situation.

The cash-flow projections will also inform you that you are likely to have excessive cash unnecessarily sitting in your account or at hand, which may be employed to earn some short-term interest.

Working capital or operating cash flow: Operating cash flow, often referred to as working capital, is the cash flow generated from internal operations. It comes from sales of the product or service of your business, and because it is generated internally, it is under your control.

Investment of Cash: Investing cash flow is generated internally from nonoperating activities. This includes investments in plants and equipment or other fixed assets, nonrecurring gains or losses, or other sources and uses of cash outside of normal operations. This excess cash must be invested correctly so that there is a reasonable return, and the principal is available when needed.

Summary of Chapter 21

Cash Flow Secrets

- Positive cash flow does not always mean profits.
- Negative cash flow does not always mean a loss.
- Cash flow projections are the best management tool for any business.

Chapter 22
Break-even Analysis

"Paying the bills": The concept of paying the bills or breakeven may be applied to any business. For entrepreneurs though, this is a powerful tool to understand and use. It gives anyone a clear picture, as to at what revenue, production, or occupancy level the business is starting to make money. This will mean that the business may be producing some revenue, but that much revenue may not be enough to pay for the fixed and variable expenses or as it is colloquially called "paying the bills" in layman's language. And it only after paying the bills, that the business may start making some profits for the owner to take home to pay for his bread and butter.

Break-even point: There are many ways for a beginner entrepreneur to keep the business on the right track and to remain aware continuously as to where it is heading. One of these tools is a simple mathematical formula, as mentioned above, which tells you at what point in revenue stream you are definitely paying all your bills. This means that the revenues are enough to pay for all the "fixed" and "variable" expenses of the business, which is also called overheads. This is called the break-even point of the business. Any revenue beyond the breakeven point will generate the profits for the business.

Break-even point must be continuously reviewed and updated, as the business grows and the circumstances in which the business is operating changes. Any change in the manufacturing volume, revenue generation, and increase or decrease of expenses, will change the break-even point.

Projection of Break-Even point: It is a simple truth, which may even sound too simplistic, that all the revenue is not profit. From the said revenue, values of goods and services have to be recovered or paid first. Therefore, if the business is a retail business, the cost of goods plus the business costs have to be added to come to total expenses. This total expense includes fixed costs or overheads and relevant variable expenses. The entrepreneur is usually able to project how much goods he needs to sell to collect such profits to cover his costs and "pay his bills." In short, the break-even point is reached when the generated revenue equals to all the fixed and relevant variable expenses so that it pays for all the business costs.

For a start-up business, it is extremely important to know this. This can be projected even before the business comes in operation. It will require some basic information about the possible fixed and variable expenses of the business. Once you have a pretty good idea of these factors, it will provide you with the information as to how much revenue needs to be generated, so as to produce enough profits to pay the ongoing expenses related to running your business.

Fixed and variable costs: To calculate the breakeven point, you will need to identify your fixed and variable costs. Fixed costs are expenses that do not vary with sales volume, such as rent, insurance, interest or cost of capital, or administrative salaries. These costs have to be paid regardless of sales, which may be less or more, or even none, and are often referred to as overhead costs. Variable costs, as its name suggests, vary directly proportionate to the sales volume, such as the costs of purchasing inventory, shipping, or manufacturing that product. Once you understand this concept, the formula for determining your break-even point requires no more than simple arithmetic calculations.

Examples: The concept of break-even may be easily understood if we take the example of a small business, in which there are mostly fixed expenses and not many variable expenses.

- **Trading company:** Let us take an example of a trading establishment that has a fixed expense of five thousand dollars in the shape of rent, electricity, and salaries, and almost no variable expense. If a profit of one dollar is made on each sale, it will have to make five thousand sales to cover the fixed overhead cost (expenses). Any further profit will come from the sales beyond that number of five thousand. Hence, it may be expressed in different ways. It may be said that its breakeven point is five thousand sales. If each item is sold at ten dollars, then it may be also expressed that the break-even point is at a revenue of fifty thousand dollars.

- **Motels and Hotels:** The breakeven point is expressed differently in different industries and businesses. It may be, for example, expressed as a percentage of occupancy in the motel business. For example, a motel may break even at 70% of its bed strength. This will mean that at 70% occupancy, the residual profit is just about enough to pay for all the fixed costs (and maybe some variable costs also). Therefore, if 70% of the beds are not filled, the motel will be making a loss or paying the fixed costs from its own pockets, or capital itself.

- **Manufacturing unit:** Similarly, in a manufacturing unit, the breakeven point may be expressed in terms of utilization of its capacity. For example, if the manufacturing unit has a capacity of producing one hundred thousand units, and each unit's sales price is such that if seventy thousand are sold, it covers all the fixed costs, then it may be said that the unit breaks even at 70% utilization of its capacity. If additional capacity is also used, because there is demand of the product, it will generate additional profits.

Regular usage of the break-even point: Depending on your business, your CPA or some person experienced in your line of business will explain to you how this concept may be used beneficially. This will tell you on an ongoing basis how you are fairing on any given day of the month, in a monthly cycle of business. With a simple setup, you may know on a given date during the month when you have broken even, and from then you are going to make profits to keep.

Ways to Lower Break-Even: Once you have understood this principle, you can make an effort to lower the break even of your business, in an intelligent way. These will then generate management decisions to achieve higher profits.

- Lower the costs. This will raise the gross margin. You need to be more careful about the cost of goods, inventory control, or decrease the labor cost by increasing the productivity. You may also lower your fixed costs to lower the break even.

- Raise prices. Sometime it takes a lot of courage to increase prices. There is always a fear of competition, who may take away your customers.

The eventual goal of any business is profit: You are in business to make a profit not just break even, but by knowing what is your break even number, you can start expecting profit, by beating that number.

Break-Even Analysis: This may be done in any business, by applying the knowledge that we have acquired so far. Your CPA should be able to help you in creating a simple tool, which may be fine tuned every so often to arrive at the break even in your business. And then of course beat that and start making the profits.

Visual understanding of the components of Break–Even analysis:

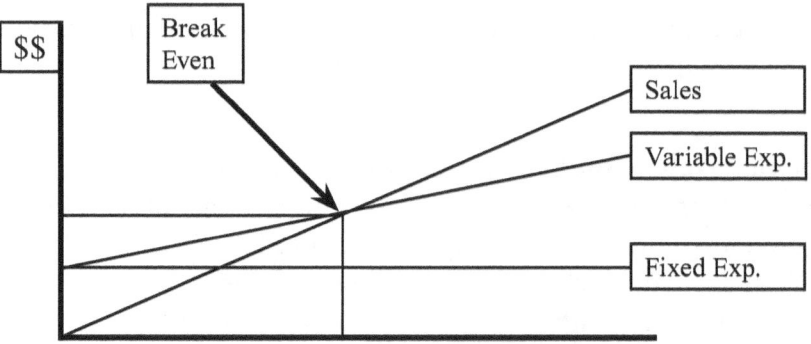

As you would see in this very simple example, there are certain fixed costs. And when they are met with by the sales, the variable expenses needs to be paid also. When both these expenses are paid, it is called Break-Even point. And beyond this point the business is said to be making profit for the entrepreneur.

If the sales are not enough to pay for all the fixed costs, and also the relevant variable costs, the business is still below the Break-

Even point, and will be making losses, although it may be producing revenues.

Section Five

Everyday-Life "Wisdoms"

Chapter 23
Your Credit Score:
Prudence Will Raise It

It is becoming increasingly important to have an acceptable credit record. Whether we like it or not, society increasingly equates the ability to manage credit responsibly with responsible behavior. Credit scoring has become one of the important tools in today's industrialized world. It attempts to provide an insight into a borrower's past financial activities in terms of repayment of borrowing they have made in the past. Based on the past record on the credit repayment history, the credit report is now being regularly used by many to predict how that individual will behave if any further credit will be extended to him.

The credit score has become a tool of primary importance for everyone in the lending industry, in particular, and in almost all businesses in general. On some occasions, however, it may become an unnecessary hurdle for persons who are only starting their journey in business and borrowing for their personal needs or business. These people will be at the disadvantage of having no credit history to predict what their future behavior will be. The credit score may also not be fair sometimes to those who fall prey to unfortunate situations and develop a bad credit record, sometimes through no fault of their own.

Credit report information: who uses it? Landlords often look at applicants' credit records before renting apartments to see whether they manage their finances responsibly and are therefore likely to pay their rent on time. Vendors use this tool to decide if they should extend a credit to their customers. Banks and other lenders look at the credit records of loan applicants to find out whether they are likely to have loans repaid. Some employers also look at credit records, especially in environments where employees handle money, and view a good credit record as a measure of maturity and stability. Insurance companies also have started using credit scoring in conjunction with their other methods of evaluation of the risk covering and arriving at a decision as to what will be an appropriate premium to be charged for covering that risk.

It is widely used by the consumer-item lenders of cars, household goods, store credit cards, and bank credit cards. Hence, these credit reports consist of the bulk of those consumer items' repayment history. Lately, the home-mortgage lenders have been using this system in one way or another in almost all the cases they are able to lend on. Similarly, almost all the lenders like banks or commercial lenders use the credit score as the first prequalifying step as to whether or not the applicant is creditworthy or not for further processing of the loan request.

Predictive value of the credit score: The reasons behind the predictive value of credit scores appear to be behavioral. The character trait that leads to careful money management seems to show up in other daily situations in which people have to make decisions about how to act, such as driving. People who manage money carefully may be more likely to have their car serviced at appropriate times and may also more effectively manage the most important financial asset most Americans own (e.g., their house), making routine repairs before they become major insurance losses. Hence, banks want such a predictive "crystal ball" to evaluate a loan application, and the insurance companies need it to foresee the possibility of loss claims in the coverage that they are providing through an insurance policy.

FICO score: Credit scoring by all credit bureaus is based on FICO scoring. FICO is an acronym that stands for Fair, Isaac & Company, a California firm founded in 1956 by Bill Fair and Earl Isaac. They created a unique credit scoring system called the FICO scoring system. Credit scoring is developed as a method of determining the likelihood as to how the credit users will pay their obligations. Since its inception, gradually but surely the credit scoring system gained tremendous popularity amongst lenders as a reliable means of credit evaluation of borrowers.

Computation of the credit score in a single three-digit number is done by complicated formulas and equations, which take into account many factors about the individual as to how he/she has behaved while repaying the credit extended to them. Credit scores are calculated by using scoring models and mathematical tables that assign points for different pieces of information that have been found to best predict future credit handling by that person. Developing these models involves studying how millions of people have used and repaid the credit extended to them. Score models are developed by credit bureaus to find predictive factors in the data that have proven to indicate future credit performance. They own the methodology, formulas, and equations used by the credit bureaus to arrive at a final three-digit score, and that being their property, it is not shared with anyone.

Elements used for arriving at a FICO score: Credit scores analyze a borrower's credit history considering numerous factors, as explained below.

- **Timely repayment of loans and bills:** One of the most important elements is the regularity of the repayment of any obligation. This may be to lenders, car-financing companies, utility companies, mall retailers, credit-card companies, and the likes. They all report to the credit bureaus if their payments are obtained in time or if late. How late? Any nonpayment or regular late payment lowers the score considerably.

- **Amount of outstanding debt versus your repayment capability:** Everyone has a different earning capacity and, hence, a different repayment capability. One of the factors taken into account in the score calculation is the relationship between these two important facts of anyone's life. As this relationship worsens (e.g., if the income goes down and debt goes up), the score goes down with it.

- **Number of open accounts:** As one starts buying some items on credit, the number of accounts that need to be paid every month increases. The number of borrowings that are still to be paid is one of the factors in calculation. The larger the number, the lower the score.

- **Frequency of application for credits:** The number of times one has applied for credit or a credit card is also one of the factors in calculation and will reduce the score.

- **The amount of time credit has been established:** The credit score gets built gradually as the feedback from the lender is reported as to how the borrower is fulfilling his obligations. As the good behavior of the borrower continues, the score gets higher.

- **The amount of credit used versus the amount of credit available:** Some people have a lot of credit cards with different credit limits. The usage of these limits against how much is still available is also a part of this equation.

- **Owning a house and length of stay therein:** If a borrower owns a house and has been living there for a considerable period of time, it shows that he is stable and, hence, the score would go higher.

- **Employment history:** Relative reliability and permanency of employment makes the score go higher.

- **Negative credit information such as bankruptcies, charge-offs, collections, etc.:** The negative information is detrimental to the score, and it stays on record for a long period of time.

Interpretation of score numbers: All the above factors and facts are combined through complicated formulas and equations, which culminates into your credit score. This score is ultimately a three-digit score between 300 and 950. The higher the score, the better the credit rating. The score is generally considered to be high enough if it is above 680. A person with that score is considered to be a "low risk" or "prime" borrower. If someone's score is below 680, it is considered to be "sub-prime" and fall in the middle category in terms of risk of lending. Any score below 560 is considered to be very low, and that person is considered to be a "poor credit risk." While a prime score is a good risk, a sub-prime score doesn't mean you should not or that you will not get a loan. In such circumstances, however, the lending institution will want to charge a higher interest rate with the stringent condition to compensate them for accommodating a loan request from a poor-risk borrower and satisfy them of repayment of loan.

Credit bureaus: Your credit score is kept and offered by mainly the three credit bureaus, namely Equifax, TransUnion, and Experian. They collect such information on almost everyone having to borrow at any point in their working life. All three of the bureaus offer FICO credit scores using the formula developed by Fair, Isaac & Company, but they each give the scores a different name. At Equifax, the FICO is known as the "Beacon" credit score. At TransUnion, it is called "Empirica." At Experian, it is called "Experian/Fair, Isaac Risk Model." Hence, in reality, there are really three FICO scores computed by data received by each of the three bureaus for each person. These scores may be slightly different when computed by these different credit bureaus. Some lenders use one of these three scores, while other lenders may use the average of three scores.

All three bureaus do not necessarily share the same data; hence, the credit score that you may be assigned by each of them may be slightly different. For example, one bureau may list more accounts for you than another, and the differences in types of accounts, payment histories, credit limits, and balances will be reflected in the score that the bureau computes about you.

Living in a country like the U.S., where the credit scoring is so frequently used by lenders, it is important to understand the factors that may improve your score or affect it adversely. You may not be able to impact and change your score in the short run. However, a constant watch on what you do and prudence that you observe, as indicated in following paragraphs, will help improve your score and will also help in avoiding those things and activities that might affect your score adversely.

Factors that will help improve your credit score:

- **Pay your bills on time.** Late payments and collections, called delinquency, always have a serious negative impact on your score. Payment history on accounts includes credit cards, retail accounts (department-store credit cards), installment loans, finance company accounts, and mortgage loans.

- **Do not apply for credit frequently.** Having a large number of inquiries on your credit report can reduce your score.

- **Reduce your credit-card balances.** If you are utilizing the maximum allowed credit on your credit cards, it will affect your credit score negatively. Your current amount of indebtedness carries a 30% weightage in the score. Having available credit actually helps your ratio of debt to available credit. If you have a credit card with a very small balance and no late pays, it looks very good, as it shows that you are able to manage your credit responsibly.

- **Obtain additional credit facility if you have limited credit.** Not having sufficient credit can also negatively impact your score.

- **Fix errors in your report.** It is your right to know what is being presented to any would-be lender about your credit, particularly if the decision is made against you and is based on that report. You need to go through the report and try and fix all the errors and other factors as enumerated above to try and bring the score as high as possible. It also makes good sense to check your credit history that is being given to your lenders once in awhile. Many lenders take the average score from the three bureaus when making their decisions, so fixing errors in all three reports before you shop for a loan may be a prudent move.

Factors that will affect your credit score adversely:

- **You have too many open accounts.** It's true that having too many open accounts can hurt your score. However, once you've opened the accounts, the damage has been done. Now you may keep them paid on time, which is the best you can do to get some benefit from those open accounts. Shutting down those accounts may not help; in fact, it may harm. The credit score looks at the difference between your available credit and what you're using. If you shut down accounts, and your total available credit shrinks, it will make your outstanding balances look larger and will hurt your score. The score also tracks the length of your credit history. Shutting older accounts can also make your credit history look younger than it actually is, which can hurt your score. Rather than closing accounts, pay down your credit-card debt. That's something that actually can and usually will improve your score. How many accounts are open, and how many have balances? A large number of open accounts, even with small balances, can indicate a higher risk of overextension.

- **Too many inquiries may hurt the score.** This has 10% weightage in your score. Applying for new credit is generally what hurts your score. Ordering a copy of your own credit report or credit score doesn't count. Mass inquiries made by credit-card lenders, who are trying to decide whether to send you an offer for a preapproved card also aren't going to hurt you either, unless you actually take them up on their offers. If you want to minimize the damage from credit inquiries, make sure that when you shop for a mortgage you do so in a fairly short period of time. The FICO score treats multiple inquiries in a fourteen-day period as just one inquiry and ignores all inquiries made within thirty days prior to the day the score is computed.

- FICO handles this by treating a group of inquiries which probably represents a search for the best rate on a single loan as though it was a single inquiry (like auto or home-mortgage loan inquiries). Inquiries are typically seen as a request for credit, and thus are factored as if you are searching for credit. Every time you fill out one of those credit-card applications to get a free hat or some gift that is offered to fill in the form, you are also clocking up an additional inquiry. Every time you fill out an online application for a credit card or other type of loan, you are adding an inquiry. Too many inquiries look bad and lower the score.

Delinquencies, bankruptcies, and collections: Previous credit performance (payment history) carries a 35% weightage in the scoring. Collection items and public records include judgments, bankruptcies, suits, liens, collection items, and wage attachments including specific details on late and missed payments. Negative information/late pays are determined using three factors:

How old is delinquency? How long ago did the last delinquency happen? How old is the late pay? A thirty-day late payment made just a month ago will affect your score much more than a ninety-day late payment from five years ago.

How bad is the delinquency? What level of delinquency was reached? How late was the payment made? Thirty days, sixty days, ninety days, or worse? Is the payment still outstanding?

How often have you defaulted? How many credit obligations have been delinquent? What is the amount of negative items as compared to your total amount of available credit? For instance, five accounts showing three late payments are much worse than ten accounts showing four late payments. One of the biggest sub-factors is how many accounts show no late payments. A good track record on most of your credit accounts will increase an overall FICO score substantially.

Chapter 13 is the kind of bankruptcy that requires a repayment plan and is looked at somewhat more favorably than a Chapter 7, which allows you to erase many of your unsecured debts. You might still be able to qualify for a loan from one of these lenders, although your interest rates will almost certainly be higher than if you had perfect credit. Collections or other judgments will certainly reduce your score, and you must avoid them with all efforts.

Length of your credit history: This has a 15% weightage in the credit score. Most often, the longer the credit history you have, the better your score. However, this factor only makes up a small percentage of your total score, so even young people, students, or others with short histories can still score high overall, as long as the other factors look good. If you are new to credit then there is little you can do to improve this part of your score. Open an account and be patient. The age of your oldest account and the average age of all your accounts are taken into consideration. How long has it been since you used certain accounts as well as the mix of older and new trade lines?

Types of outstanding credit: This has a weightage of 10% in the computation of your credit score. You should never open accounts you don't intend to use anyway. Your score takes into account what type and how many accounts you have. The optimal ratio of installment versus revolving accounts depends on your profile and differs from person to person. One factor that seems to have significant influence is your installment loans. Too many can lower this portion of your score, since that is a recurrent obligation against your income every month.

General guidelines on reading credit score: Generally the credit score is looked upon as the first indicator and the reader draws the following inference from this information about the status of your credit:

Excellent: Above 750
Good: Below 749 but higher than 660.
Fair: Below 659 but higher than 620.
Poor: Below 619.

As explained in detail in this chapter, the credit score by itself is not the only indicator of the health of your credit. The lender would look at many other factors to finally interpret the status of your credit.

Summary of Chapter 23

Credit Score

Credit Bureaus provide **FICO** scores.

- Equifax produces **Beacon Score**.
- Trans Union produces **Empirical Score**.
- Experian produces **"Experian/Fair, Isaac Risk Model."**

How to Fine Tune your Credit Score

Increase your Credit Score:
- Pay your bills on time.
- Keep borrowing to minimum.
- Have minimal open accounts.
- Don't apply for credit frequently.
- Create long employment history.
- Check and fix your credit history records with the bureaus.

Following will Decrease your Credit Score:
- Negative Credit Information.
    - Charge offs
    - Collections
    - Bankruptcy
- Tardy Payment History.
- Many Applications for Credit.
- Many Open Accounts.

Chapter 24

Limited-Liability Entities:
Careful Planning Helps

General: The U.S. is the most litigious country. It is obvious from the fact that the U.S. has the highest concentration of attorneys in the whole world. Sometimes litigation may be based on some frivolous and flimsy reason. On most occasions, though, there is a genuine grievance, which becomes the cause of action. The most common causes of litigations are for damages called for negligence, breach of contracts, or other obligations, including credit extension and its nonpayment.

In any business, intent is everything: The lending business is based on trust and trustworthiness. It is absolutely essential that anyone desirous of being in business for an extended period of time has to have good intentions about fulfilling his/her obligations. In the business world, it is rare to find an intentionally fraudulent borrowing, wherein the borrower planned not to pay back the obligations, although such schemes and scams are possible. The business cannot last very long if other counterparts of the business, like vendors, suppliers, or creditors, sense even the slightest malafide intention of the owner of the business. Thus, one may generalize that, by and large, the intention of the borrower is good when he applies for a loan and creates an obligation.

Circumstances beyond control: Sometimes, despite having good intentions, the business owner is unable to pay back the loan obligation due to some genuine reasons beyond his/her own control. These reasons may be a sudden downturn in the economy or a particular bad spot in an industry when the expected payments are not received and, hence, payment obligations cannot be met.

Such a state of affairs may put a business in a cash-flow bind for a short term, and if the losses pile up, the cash flow becomes negative and may stay negative. If this is not corrected soon, or if some alternative facility for the required finances is not arranged soon to revert the cash flow and make business healthy to be profitable again, the payment obligations may not be fulfilled.

In such a situation, the business owners or executives may not be directly or on many occasions even indirectly responsible for the problems occurring with that business. However, the creditors may push a well-intentioned business into liquidation under these circumstances. This, in turn, may put the business owner in line for owning the business debts and, consequently, he may be forced to file a personal bankruptcy also.

Objective and usage of limited-liability entities: Capitalist and industrialized countries like the U.S. are based on free enterprise. However, most of the time, the entrepreneurs have no experience of the business. Therefore the limited-liability entities are an attempt to create a mechanism whereby the entrepreneur is assured that while trying out his ideas, he may lose all the liquidity that he has employed in the business, but he may not lose his basic worldly possessions, like his house, car, clothing, and so forth. Such a reassurance encourages the entrepreneurial spirit, so that they are not discouraged to try out their ideas, worrying about losing everything. Such an arrangement allows the nation to try out many good innovations that otherwise would have been lost, because they are never put to test. So, basically, these limited-liability entities protect the entrepreneurs from personal liabilities. Over the course of last century, many laws have been reformed to this end. Legislature have enacted laws to provide protection to the owners of businesses from personal liabilities through these entities.

These limited-liability entities are treated as natural persons in the eyes of the law. The structure that is set up is such that the liability of that entity is to the extent of the equity or capital that has been contributed by the shareholders or members into it. The shareholder may have many other assets outside that entity, but that is not looked upon legally as chargeable against the obligations created by that entity. Thus, the concept and purpose of limited-liability entities is to protect the business owner or executive from personal bankruptcy if the business controlled by a limited-liability entity goes into liquidation. Hence, the shareholders and owners are not responsible any further or in addition to the equity that they have contributed in the entity. Such laws are being adopted more and more in the rest of the industrialized world and even in third-world countries to encourage investors and entrepreneurs.

Choosing the structure of your business: You may operate your business or organization under any one of several organizational structures. Each type of structure has certain advantages and disadvantages that should be considered. You should contact an attorney, accountant, financial advisor, banker, or other business or legal advisors to determine which form is most suitable for your business or organization. One important aspect is the tax breaks that such entities enjoy. These entities should be created preferably with the help of an attorney or your CPA, although some persons like to complete the necessary formalities and paperwork themselves.

A sole proprietorship is one individual in business alone. Sole proprietorship has been the most common form of business structure. This type of business is simple to form and operate and may enjoy greater flexibility of management and fewer legal controls. However, the business owner is personally liable for all debts incurred by the business.

A general partnership is composed of two or more persons who agree to contribute money, labor, and/or skill to a business. Each partner shares the profits, losses, and management of the business, and each partner is personally and equally liable for debts of the partnership. Formal terms of the partnership are usually contained in a written partnership agreement.

Different types of limited-liability entities: If the liability is even a slightest concern, the above two structures are not advisable to be used. And in the new environment of so many litigations, more and more people are preferring and are being advised to work through limited-liability entities.

There are several limited-liability entities available to choose from in different scenarios and situations. One important fact that needs to be repeated is that these entities are seen as natural persons in the eyes of the law, and the owners are seen as employees of such entities, working as officers or managers. We shall just describe some salient features of each of them here.

Limited partnership (LP): LP at the end of the name of the business recognizes this entity. As the definition indicates, the difference between a limited partnership and a general partnership is that a limited partnership has two classes of partners: general and limited.

An LP is composed of one or more general partners and one or more limited partners. The general partners manage the business and share in its profits and losses. Limited partners share in the profits of the business, but their losses are limited to the extent of their investment. Limited partners are usually not involved in the day-to-day operations of the business, and they also do not have control over daily decisions made for the business, which is the responsibility and prerogative of the general partners only. Upon dissolution, a limited partner has priority over a general partner in asset distribution. Although the limited partnership is not obliged to file a partnership agreement with the Secretary of State in all states, a written partnership agreement is recommended.

A limited-liability partnership: This is similar to a general partnership except that, normally, a partner does not have personal liability for the negligence of another partner. This business structure is used most commonly by professionals such as accountants and lawyers.

A corporation is a more complex business structure. As a chartered legal entity, a corporation has certain rights, privileges, and liabilities beyond those of an individual. Doing business as a corporation may yield tax or financial benefits, but these can be offset by other considerations, such as licensing fees or decreased personal control. Corporations may be formed for profit or nonprofit purposes. This is the most commonly used traditional entity. They are generally supposed to indicate their limited liability by showing "Corporation" or "Inc" at the end of their names. Corporations may have any number of shareholders from one to an unlimited number. Each person's shareholding shows their equity contribution and profit and loss exposure. This may be run as a regular, or C, corporation. However, the shareholders may elect to be a subchapter S corporation or a closed corporation to suit their own circumstances. A subchapter S corporation may not have more than seventy-five shareholders, and all of them have to be citizens or legal residents of the U.S. Regular, or C, or S corporations are similar so far as their limitation of liability of shareholders is concerned.

A regular C corporation pays its own taxes and then may or may not distribute the remaining profit. Closed, or S, corporations are very popular for small businesses. Once the election of subchapter S is done, the corporation is not obliged to pay the corporate taxes. All profits and losses, and, hence, the tax liability, flows through to the shareholders' personal returns. Therefore, S corporations are also called flow-through corporations. Nonresident aliens are not eligible for S corporation status. The corporations will have shareholders, officers, and a board of directors. In a typical stock corporation, the shareholders elect directors, and the directors vote for officers.

The limited-liability company (LLC) is the newest form of business structure allowed to be formed and approved by the IRS. An LLC is formed by one or more individuals or entities through a special written agreement. The agreement details the organization, including provisions for management, assignability of interests, and distribution of profits or losses. Limited-liability companies are permitted to engage in any lawful, for-profit business or activity other than banking or insurance. These indicate their limited-liability status by writing LLC at the end of their names. Its usefulness in limiting liability is still being viewed with caution by some because of these not having been tested comprehensively in the courts of law. An LLC acts in many ways like an S corporation but without many of its paperwork hassles. It can split earnings and ownership percentages. The IRS allows its treatment as a partnership or a corporation. The LLC is governed by a contract called an operating agreement. These companies will have equity-contributing members and managers to look after the day-to-day affairs of company.

Summary of Chapter 24

<u>Business Entities</u>

- Proprietorship

- Partnership

- Limited Liability Entities

  - Corporations

    - "S" corporations

    - "C" corporations

  - Limited Liability Partnerships

    - Limited Partners

    - General Partners

  - Limited Liability Company

Chapter 25
Franchising Wisdom: Buying the Experience at a Price

Objective of pursuing a franchise business: This may be narrated in one simple sentence: a franchised business is like buying someone else's experience of a successful and proven concept along with their ongoing support and supervision. Almost every entrepreneur reaches a point when he needs to decide whether he goes on his own or becomes a part of a franchise. A franchise has many advantages for a beginner but may not be suitable for every entrepreneur. Hence, this question needs to be answered by the individual on case-to-case basis. The only way to come up with an intelligent answer is to look at the relative advantages and disadvantages of each approach.

What is a Franchise? A franchise is a legal and contractual binding between a franchisor and a franchisee. This contract or agreement is drawn for the franchisee to be able to benefit from the commercial relationship between the owner of a trademark or advertising symbol, and someone seeking the right to use that identification in a business. The franchise format is used in many different industries, ranging from accounting and advertising to vending and water conditioning.

Advantages of franchising:

- **It is a success story.** There are an estimated 1,500 franchise companies doing business through more than 320,000 retail units in the U.S. This in itself tells the success story of the franchised business. In addition, there are 75 industries that use franchising to distribute goods and services to consumers.

- **You do not need to reinvent the wheel.** There are many significant advantages to franchisees. The experience that the original business has gained from making a lot of mistakes is avoided by joining a franchise. This is perhaps the biggest pitfall, which may be very costly for an entrepreneur in terms of time, money, and energy, if he is on his own and has to learn from his own mistakes. They benefit from the franchisor's experience and expertise, so they don't have to "reinvent the wheel" in their own venture. Most franchise systems spring from a successful business that has been operated by an owner who is interested in expanding its reach. All or most of the problems likely to be encountered by any individual unit in the franchise have already been met and resolved by the original business. Hence, in effect, the franchisor has a template for a successful business, and it uses that template to replicate its success from location to location.

- **You have name and logo recognition.** The franchisors have name recognition through their logos. They also have a large budget for advertising, which helps the franchisees significantly. Potential customers are more likely to be familiar with the name, brand, or trademark of a franchise system than that of an independent business. Consumers know they can go into any franchised fast-food outlet or coffee shop, for example, and expect the same quality of product and service they get at their hometown outlet. That consistency of product, quality, service, and brand identity is one of the major advantages of owning a franchise.

- **A franchise is a business in a box.** Buying a franchise is like buying a business in a box. A franchise is a known quantity with an existing brand identity. A new franchise business has the potential to establish a customer base much more quickly than a comparable independent business. As a result, it may begin turning a profit sooner than the independent business would.

- **It is a crown, not an individual.** Statistically, a franchise chain with hundreds of outlets managed by individual owners is going to be more successful than a similarly sized independent chain whose outlets are managed by employees who have no ownership stake in the business. This has been proved in practice many times around.

- **You receive management support.** Franchising allows the operator to concentrate on the day-to-day business, leaving a lot of details to be handled by the franchisor. A core concept of franchising is that the franchisor provides its franchisees with ongoing management support for the life of the franchise.

- **A franchise is a turnkey operation.** Buying a franchise is as close as you can come to buying a truly turnkey operation. The franchisee has to come up with the capital to get the business started, and he has to be willing to invest the sweat equity needed to make it a profitable venture. In terms of holding your destiny in your own hands and still having the security of a substantial safety net, franchising really does offer the best of both worlds when it comes to business ownership.

Investments: The average initial investment level for nearly eight out of ten franchises, excluding real estate, is less than $250,000. This, in itself, makes it a doable venture for many entrepreneurs. Moreover, with luck and the right approach, the lending institutions will be more favorable to allow a loan for a franchised unit, which has a history of success, instead of loaning a solo venture.

Fees: Typically, the initial franchise fees for buying the usage rights of a logo or trademark are anywhere from $10,000 to $100,000. However, the franchisor does not depend on the fees as the income. Their mainstay of income is from the royalties.

Royalties: Average royalty fees range from 3% to 8% of monthly gross sales. A good franchise company generates the bulk of its profits from the royalties paid by existing franchisees, not from the sale of a new franchise. Since those royalties are directly tied to the sales volume of the individual franchise outlets, the franchisor's success is inextricably bound to that of its franchisees. It is a wholly symbiotic system, one where each party to the deal has tremendous motivation to see the other party succeed. It is a true win-win situation, something that is quite rare in the business world.

Price to pay for franchising, or the disadvantages:

- **Strong binding of destiny of the franchisee:** Typically, having been successful, the franchisor ensures that a franchisee business is bound to follow a set of rules dictated unilaterally. This seems unfair many a time, but generally that price needs to be paid to acquire a franchise.

- **Unilateral legal binding:** While each franchisor creates its own franchise agreement or contract, those contracts are usually non-negotiable. Therefore, the franchisee has almost no room to move from the franchise agreement presented to him. It is either take it or leave it for him, which may not be acceptable to some of the independent-minded people.

- **Fees and royalties:** In return for the advantages franchisees receive from their franchisors, they pay an initial franchise fee, which is, in effect, the price of purchasing the business approval from the franchisor. Yet another ongoing fee called a royalty is based on a percentage of the franchise unit's sales and has to be paid to keep alive the arrangement of using their logo and support. Royalties run between 3% and 8% in most franchise systems, and some collect an additional 1% to 3% that is earmarked for an advertising fund.

- **Sacrificing independence:** In the franchising system, the franchisee has to sacrifice a certain amount of independence for the greater good of the franchise system. For example, while an independent business owner is free to decide that his or her business would look better with a new style of decor or a new emblem, the franchise owner has no such freedom.

American Association of Franchisees and Dealers (AAFD). There are several organizations like AAFD, which help create a better understanding between the franchisors, franchisees, and franchise attorneys. They strive to create a platform for all parties to meet on the table and stay on the same page to avoid any misunderstanding or conflicts.

Chapter 26
Wisdom about Tax Advantages of Legal Entities

When a small business becomes large: This is a good problem to have to expand, get bigger, and become more profitable. However, when the business is started by an entrepreneur, he does not know how big it will be and how quickly that will happen, if that happens.

Hence, the entrepreneur must learn to project these possibilities while starting the business. It may not seem very important on day one while starting the business. However, as the business gets expanded and the entity becomes large, the initial choice of the entity may come to help or haunt the successful businessman. Hence, it may be prudent to give thought about the choice of the entity right at the outset.

Comparison of tax savings in different entities: Legally, a lesser amount of tax may be owed and paid to Uncle Sam by choosing an appropriate entity for doing the business through.

Corporations: As mentioned earlier, corporations are considered to be a natural person in the eyes of the law. Hence, they pay the federal income tax by filing a return. Hence, in practice, the regular, or C, corporations are taxed twice: First, the corporation pays the corporate tax on the profits. Then, when the profits are distributed out to shareholders as dividends, the shareholders pay the tax again at their appropriate tax bracket.

However, the government has enacted several generous tax benefits also for corporations. Since the corporations are treated as a natural person, the owner, who may hold 100% of its shares, is an employee of that corporate entity. All the usual expenses of the business, which may include facilities for employees like cars, health insurance, traveling, and the likes, may be deducted from the profit before paying the corporate tax. This reduces the tax liability of the entity.

If "twice taxing" is a concern, there is a possibility of opting for subchapter S election. This will avoid paying the income taxes twice, since all the profits are distributed to the shareholders and no corporate tax is due on these S corporations. Since all the profit is distributed to the shareholders, it is also called a flow-through entity.

Limited partnerships (LP or Ltd) and limited-liability companies (LLCs): These are also called flow-through entities, since all the profits are distributed to its members or partners. They, in turn, include such earnings in their individual tax returns and pay the taxes at their relevant tax brackets.

Limitations to these advantages: There are certain limitations to such advantages that one may avail from these legal entities. For example, in an S Corporation, there may not be more than seventy-five stockholders, and all stockholders have to be U.S. residents. For C corporations, there are no such limitations, but there is a two-stage taxation, as explained earlier.

With regard to LLCs and limited partnerships, there are certain limitations and also advantages. These need to be understood and discussed with a CPA and/or an attorney to come to a correct decision as to which entity will be most beneficial from the tax angle and many other perspectives in the future. One important advantage worth mentioning is that if a structure is needed, wherein disproportionate investment, profits, and losses may need to be assigned, these are the correct entities to use. Corporations do not allow for such an arrangement.

Chapter 27

Bankruptcy Protection: Wisdom You Hope You Don't Need

Why bankruptcy protection? As has been mentioned earlier, any business—particularly banking and lending businesses—is based on trust and trustworthiness. It is generally presumed that everyone starts with good intentions to fulfill his obligations. Hence, a company or person who is unable to pay back his obligations may have some genuine reason for not being able to pay instead of having just a bad intention to keep the money and not pay.

There may be one or many of these reasons to cause such a situation. These include a downturn in the economy, lack of enough working capital, short-term cash-flow problem, unforeseen competition, excessive overheads, and many such reasons. If this cannot be corrected soon, or some alternative facility measures cannot be arranged, the creditors may push a well-intentioned business into liquidation or bankruptcy. This, in turn, may put the business owner/ executive in the line for owning the debts and, hence, going into filing personal bankruptcy. Presuming that the intent of the entrepreneur is good, the bankruptcy protection laws have been enacted to prevent some good businesses and their owners from being wiped off due to no mistake of their own.

History of bankruptcy protection laws: The bankruptcy provision was included by our Founding Fathers in reaction to the "debtors' prison" of colonial times, in which individuals could be imprisoned for their debts. In olden days and during British colonial rule, if a debtor did not pay his obligation, he may be put into debtors' prison, which may be a private jail created by the creditor.

However, since the year 1800, when bankruptcy laws were copied straight from the English laws, this country has had some formal bankruptcy laws off and on.

Before the twentieth century, rules and practices concerning bankruptcy generally favored the creditor and were very harsh toward the bankrupt. The focus was on recovering the investments of the creditors, and almost all bankruptcies at this time were involuntary. In England, the first official laws concerning bankruptcy were passed in 1542 under Henry VIII. A bankrupt individual was considered a criminal and was subject to criminal punishment. Potential punishments ranged from incarceration in debtors' prison to the death penalty.

The laws enacted in 1800 and 1841 in the U.S. allowed only minimal discharge of personal debt. It was in 1867 that the corporations were also included in such protection. The objective of these laws has been to allow rehabilitation or reorganization for the debtors in distress. The Bankruptcy Act of 1978 reviewed and fully reformed Chapter 11 for business reorganization and Chapter 13 for personal bankruptcy. Further reforms in 1994 included many provisions for both business and consumer bankruptcy, including provisions to expedite bankruptcy proceedings and provisions to encourage individual debtors to use Chapter 13 to reschedule their debts rather than using Chapter 7 to liquidate.

As mentioned in previous paragraphs, the basis of these laws has a strong pro-debtor ideological current and an increasingly stronger bankruptcy bar. These have been met with by a directly opposite and organized creditor lobby.

Bankruptcy in many developing countries: In most of the developing countries, the laws to govern insolvency have been enacted. However, it is ironical that in most of those third-world countries, the filing of bankruptcy is considered to be almost a social stigma and sin even today. Bankruptcy is taken to be such a black dot in a bankrupt person's life and career that he may be excommunicated and carries that stigma for his whole life. The children of that family may even find it difficult to get married because the right match will not be available in the traditional society, where many of the marriages are still arranged by elders. A person who has filed bankruptcy is looked down upon as a dishonest debtor. It may be so bad for a respected and reputable person that he may even commit suicide before telling anyone that he cannot repay his debts.

Bankruptcy in the U.S.: In the United States, filing for bankruptcy protection is an important legal right due to pro-debtor sentiments. It is a choice and an instrument for the person and business to be protected from an oppressive indebtedness caused by unforeseen sluggishness in the economy or the industry they are in, or some unforeseen event in the history of the business.

Different chapters: The Bankruptcy Code provides for five separate types of bankruptcy proceedings. Since Chapters 9 and 12 are available only to municipalities or family farmers, the remaining Chapters 7, 11, and 13 are the ones that individuals and businesses would be concerned with.

Of these, Chapter 11 and 13 are concerned with reorganization, whereas chapter 7 is liquidation supervised by the bankruptcy court.

In a typical Chapter 7 bankruptcy (also known as liquidation), a trustee collects the nonexempt property of the debtor, converts the property to cash, and distributes the cash to the creditors.

In contrast, Chapters 11, 12, and 13 of the Bankruptcy Code contemplate debtor rehabilitation. In a rehabilitation case, creditors look to future earnings of the debtor, not to the current property of the debtor. Under rehabilitation, a debtor will generally retain his assets and property while making payments to creditors pursuant to a court-approved plan.

Chapter 13 bankruptcy: A Chapter 13 bankruptcy, or "wage earner reorganization," is available only to individuals with regular income. It requires that the debtor file a plan providing for payment to creditors over a period of up to five years. The benefits of a Chapter 13 include the ability to reinstate a home mortgage that is in default, stop IRS collection efforts while payments are made, and retain personal assets.

Chapter 11 bankruptcy: Chapter 11 reorganization is available to individuals and businesses. It would legally provide individuals and businesses with an opportunity to reorganize their debts and make arrangements to pay all or a portion of the debts, or sell the business, while obtaining protection from creditors through the court of law. A Chapter 11 bankruptcy generally provides more flexibility than Chapter 13 reorganization for individuals.

Bankruptcy is the legal method for a debtor to "discharge" or relieve himself of the debts that he owes. While no debtor is guaranteed a total discharge of his debt, most debtors who file for bankruptcy are given such relief. One of the primary purposes of the Bankruptcy Act is to relieve the honest debtor from the weight of oppressive indebtedness and to provide the debtor with a fresh start. Any person can file for bankruptcy protection from creditors. In addition, most businesses and charitable organizations may also qualify for bankruptcy protection.

Chapter 28

Property Transaction Wisdom: The Ultimate Goal

At a certain point in the life of a business and its owner, there comes a stage that they need to think about owning a property. It may be right at the beginning, when some equipment may have to be bought as business assets, or it may be a real estate. A traditional business may be located in a rented premise. However, there is a general tendency for the small business to try and buy the business' real estate premises if possible. Here we shall discuss only about the real estate transaction.

Do you really want to own a property? This question needs to be answered clearly within the organization or within the family by looking at different options and priorities. You will be well advised to discuss the matter with your CPA, who will be able to paint a clear picture about the pros and cons of owning a property versus renting it for business. There are certain tax consequences, which really work against you if you own property for the business. If you still think it to be prudent to buy the business real estate, you must take your CPA in confidence to try and ensure the best route to take, particularly in terms of who should own the property: you or the business entity?

However, as soon as it is decided in principle that the business now needs to own the property to be housed in or for any other purpose, there is a chain of events that starts.

Identify broker or real estate agent You need to contact a friendly real estate agent who may patiently show you at least a few places until you find the one that suits your needs. You must also keep in mind the budget that you may have to acquire such property; hence, keep your search limited within the parameters of your budget.

Identify the property: The first step is to decide the location and size of the property. It also needs to be decided at the same time whether the business would build a property to suit its own needs or buy a built property, and if need be, remodel it to suit the needs.

Earnest-money contract: Once you have found the property and like the price, you may go through some negotiation to bring the price down within your comfort level. Once the price is agreed upon between the seller through his broker and you through your agent, an earnest-money contract has to be written up. Normally, it is recommended that you hire an attorney to do this to ensure that you do not miss any important legal steps. This is a legal contract specifying the terms and conditions to bring about the transaction. Some of the important matters it addresses are

- **Price agreed:** It specifies the price agreed by both parties. It may also include the inclusions or exclusions of some of the items, which may be on the property.

- **Earnest-money deposit:** Once the two parties agree to buy and sell, there are certain important steps in between that need to be taken by both parties to the deal, the buyer and the seller. The seller needs to take the property off the market. In return for the seller taking the property off the market and reserving it for the buyer for a certain agreed period of time, the seller will need to have an assurance of the buyer's intention. This is where earnest money comes in. This is usually kept with a third party for the safety and comfort of both parties, like in an escrow with the title company, a banker, or an attorney acceptable to both parties. Depending upon the contract, this is normally a returnable deposit, unless there is a default on the part of buyer under the terms of the contract. The amount of this deposit is negotiable, but usually 1% of the value of the property will suffice.

- **Feasibility period:** An important condition in the earnest-money contract is the feasibility period allowed to the buyer, within which he has to do what is commonly known as "due diligence." This is ascertaining that the property is in acceptable condition and that the business therein, if any, is bringing the buyer's desired revenue and, hence, the profit. The buyer will also need to ensure that the property is environmentally clean, get its appraisal value done and tentatively initiate financing he may require from the bank or any other lending institution. Normally thirty to forty-five days are allowed for this work.

- **Time to arrange financing:** All property transactions, barring a few, involve some financing from the lending institution. This procedure usually takes about sixty days. During this time the bank will have its own appraisal and environmental studies done for the property. They will also want to look at the buyer's credit score and financials. The lender would also like to scrutinize the cash flow of the buyer's entity and that of its owner or shareholder. If it is an income-generating property, the lender will also want to see the history of that business and its tax returns.

- **Closing date:** The closing, completion of the sale, or consummation of the agreement date is also tentatively agreed to and mentioned in the contract. This is the day on which the buyer and his lending institution pay the price to the seller as agreed. From then on, the buyer is owner and responsible for all the affairs of that property, including insurance and liabilities.

Although from the practical standpoint the above-mentioned are the important terms of the earnest-money contract, it must be stressed here that each and every condition in the contract is important because it is legally binding to both parties. You must review them with your attorney and make sure you do not default, since in that case your earnest money may become nonrefundable. Other terms and conditions of the contract may be

- **Seller financing:** The seller may have agreed to finance a part of the sale price, in which case other terms will be about how the balance amount will be paid, what interest it will attract, and what happens if the buyer defaults to pay the balance amount.

- **Owner's policy of title insurance:** The owner usually has to provide the title insurance of the property that he is selling, meaning the title is clear and that he has an insurance against any issue about it arising in future.

- **Prorating of all dues of taxes and utilities:** Until the date of sale, the seller is responsible for all these expenses. If the closing is in the middle of the month, these expenses will have to be prorated between the buyer and the seller and reconciled at closing with an adjustment in payment owed by the buyer.

- **General warranty deed is to be recorded at buyer's expense conveying a good and marketable title:** This has to be done at the closing, so that the buyer, who has now paid the seller off, becomes an absolute owner of the property.

- **Restrictive covenants, rights of parties in possession, and discrepancies in title** may need to be sorted out and agreed upon by both parties before the closing.

- **In case of default by either party,** the seller may enforce specific performance by the buyer or keep the earnest-money amount as liquidated damages; whereas, the buyer may seek specific performance or any other relief or remedy as allowed by the law.

Need of an attorney: It must be stressed here that this is only a summary of what goes on at the time of buying any real estate. This may be termed as the common sense of property transaction. Any would-be buyer of real estate or any property must be aware of this at the minimum. Under all circumstances it is strongly advised and recommended that you hire an attorney experienced in real estate deals to ensure that your legal interest is well looked after.

Summary of Chapter 28

Buying a Property for Business Purposes

Do you really need to buy the property for your business? If so:

- Identify Realtor
- Identify Property
- Agree at a Price
    - Who will pay for title insurance policy?
- Write Earnest Money Contract
- Feasibility Period for due diligence
- Arrange Financing
    - Sellers financing or
    - Institutional financing
- Closing the deal
    - General warranty deed

Chapter 29

Will and Estate Planning Wisdom: a Must for All

Having a will drawn and arranging estate planning are two different but related subjects. We shall discuss them one by one.

Why would anyone need to draw a will? Almost everyone, when he/she passes away from this world, leaves certain assets in their own name. Usually, the owner has a pretty good idea who those assets should go to. However, this can only happen if the deceased has drawn a will during his lifetime to declare his wish about the disposal of his assets. Hence, it is imperative that everyone has a written will in place to indicate what he wishes to be done with the assets that are left behind. No matter what the size of the asset, it is only prudent to have this drawn up in one's lifetime for several good reasons.

The will must also be revised as necessary when one's financial worth changes, and the social and familial circumstances change. This will ensure distribution of your assets after your death to your desired persons only and not according to the state's generic formula, wherein your hard-earned assets may be distributed to some heirs that you do not even know.

It is a legal instrument to tell the whole world as to what you would like done with your estate when you pass away and are absent from the scene. And it is only prudent to have such a will in place whether you have small estate or a large one, so that its distribution is according to your desire.

Distribution of assets during your lifetime: Ideally, one should distribute all of his assets during his lifetime, before death, to someone he likes, loves, and cares for. However, it is not always practical to do so. One does not know how long one has left to live and what he will need during the remaining time. If all the assets are distributed, and if it is lost by the recipient in losses in business or hobbies, there will be nothing left for the person to be looked after for the remainder of his life. Even if it is not lost, the recipient may not take care of the distributor as nicely as the distributor may have wished. Hence for such eventuality, some residual assets may have been left in the name of deceased, even though he may have distributed most of it during his lifetime.

Distribution of assets after death: Although most of the assets may have been distributed, some will be left in the name of the dead person. The leftover personal property and/or real property, which, when combined, is called an **estate**, is a net asset after satisfying all the liabilities. This remains in the name of the deceased, which needs to be distributed.

Probate: This is the state's legal procedure for handling two major functions for your estate. First is identification of the rightful heirs to the estate and the share that each heir will receive. Second is getting the legal title of the property transferred from your name "(now deceased)", into the name of the legal heirs. This is the function of the court. Therefore, if you have a will already available, the first function is done, and the second is only a matter of procedure. However, if a will is not in place, the finding of the proper heir may be slow and expensive and may eat away a large portion of the asset itself.

Distribution of assets after death with a will present: For a distribution of the estate as per the desire of the deceased, one needs to have a will written during the lifetime and kept in safe place, so that instead of following some formula evolved by the lawmakers, your assets are distributed according to your "will" even after you pass away.

If the entire asset is still in the name of the deceased, it has to pass through the process of probate. However, the probate is easiest, though not avoidable, if a will is present. If the deceased has a will drawn during his lifetime, it makes it easier to distribute the asset, since the heirs and their shares are all identified in the will. The only work in probate is the transfer of the legal title of the property.

A will has to be written, signed, and kept with someone reliable who will make it available when needed. The maker of will normally appoints an executor of the will who then looks after proper distribution of the assets to persons as desired by the deceased. The executor has to take this on as a fiduciary responsibility and has to carry it out properly as per the laws of the state.

Distribution of assets after death without a will: The legislators elected by the public created some generic guidelines to dispose the estate of a dead person if he has not drawn a will during his lifetime to declare his wishes as to how to dispose his leftover assets. However, those generic formulas may not be what you may have in mind for the disposal of your assets. In the absence of a will, the court appoints a trustee, who decides the rightful heir as per the law. He tries to find them and then transfers the titles of the property in their name. This process is slow and expensive and, hence, one may repeat once more that everyone must have a written will before the death.

Estate Planning: Estate planning is generally considered to be essential if one is likely to leave behind a large asset say, over a million dollars. The objective of discussing this subject is to provide some general knowledge about this legal instrument. It is more for awareness of its availability, if needed, so that one may take care of one's personal assets in a prudent manner.

Estate planning is a vast subject—so much so that some attorneys and financial consultants practice only this specialty all their life. Hence, a few pages written here can only provide some general knowledge and important facts that everyone should know.

Estate planning is required by a person with fairly high net worth who wishes to legally avoid the estate tax and use all the relief available under law to be able to do so. An entrepreneur may not be a very high-net-worth individual in the beginning, but hopefully with success and hard work he will acquire a lot of wealth and, at that time, the understanding of this subject will come in handy. The law keeps on changing in allowing the dollar amount of exempted assets and, hence, a current situation in law has to be ascertained to see if this planning is necessary for you or not.

Estate-planning instruments: This is a specialized subject, and we shall only touch upon some salient features. To plan this, you need an experienced estate-planning attorney and CPA to do a good job.

If you transfer all your assets into some entity, which remains alive after your passing away, you then avoid the probate almost altogether. These entities may be any one or a combination of the following:

Family estate planning entities may a

- Living trust

- Life estate trust

- Family limited partnership

Avoidance of tax and probate by using trust as a vehicle: The way a trust avoids probate is by titling your property in the name of the trust before your death. You have complete control of the property during your life, but the trust is considered to be the legal owner of the property for title-transfer purposes. Upon your death, a trustee that you pre-selected will simply handle the transfers or payments to your heirs that you specified in the trust. You have a great deal of flexibility in specifying the details of these payments and transfers. After your death, the trustee can handle everything quickly and simply without lawyers, court supervision, or excessive costs and delays.

Other advantages of trust: A trust will have some other advantages also, which are as follows:

- Management of the estate during mental incapacitation: When the assets are placed in a trust as sole owner, it is a good vehicle to ensure that your assets are well taken care of in all different ways through the trustee, in case of mental incapacitation of the maker of trust

- Probate avoidance: As mentioned earlier, if the assets are held by the trust, a probate process is eliminated.
- Reduction or elimination of death taxation: Since the assets are held by the trust legally, the assets do not attract the death taxes at the time of the passing away of the owner.

- Controlled transfer of estate to proper heirs: The trust will be a good vehicle to have the transfer of the assets you have listed for disposal be carried out by the trustee and per your will.

- Protecting the estate from lawsuits and seizures: Since the assets are in the trust, it may not be reached by the lawsuits against the owner and liabilities arising from there.

Chapter 30
Adequate Insurance Wisdom: You Can't Overinsure

Why insure? Ensuring that you have adequate insurance coverage is an absolute necessity in our daily life. Every entrepreneur makes money through hard work. The assets so collected need to be insured against unforeseen circumstances and natural disasters. Apart from the assets earned, life itself is an asset. Many times the lender lends to you only if he thinks that you are experienced, and healthy. God forbid, if your health dwindles or you meet with a maiming or fatal accident one of the foremost worries for the lender is how to get his loan paid under such circumstances. To obviate such an eventuality, the lender will want to have your life insured to pay the loan, just in case. This is now becoming a regular requirement by the lender.

Different kinds of insurance: While talking about insurance, people all kinds of things and there are insurance companies who are ready to accept the risk of sometime exotic and unusual items. Nevertheless, usual risks that need to be covered in daily life are life, health, automobile, home (including its contents), and commercial insurance covering the premises, inventory, and third-party liability are the main ones. On top of these, many high-net-worth individuals also carry an "umbrella" insurance to take care of any unforeseen claims that may not have been covered under their usual insurance coverage. It goes without mentioning here that adequate insurance is a necessity, despite its seemingly unnecessary expense. One of our wealthy and successful friends says, "You cannot overinsure yourself." Such is the importance of adequate insurance coverage. This is only prudent, as many experienced people will agree.

Life insurance: This is a common method used to collect a savings. It also helps prepare for unforeseen events if someone dies with responsibilities to be fulfilled. The premium depends upon the actuary's tables. There are many products to choose from. The main two are term insurance and whole life insurance. These are ways used to protect the savings from liabilities by creating trusts, which also helps avoid estate taxes.

Insurance underwriting: This is a term very frequently used in the insurance industry. Again, the purpose of the underwriting process is the same or similar to ensure that the risk that the insurance company is about to carry is fairly priced with an appropriate premium. Hence, the underwriters in the insurance industry try to forecast or project the possibility of a loss claim in the policy that is being issued. Insurance underwriters use a similar but perhaps more sophisticated system, which is a combination of the credit score and information from claim databases.

Insurance scores: These are confidential rankings based on credit-history information and CLUE reports, which are explained below. They are a measure of how a person manages his or her financial affairs. As mentioned earlier, people who manage their finances well tend to also manage other important aspects of their lives responsibly. Combined with factors such as geographical area, previous accidents, age and gender, insurance scores enable insurers to price more accurately, so that people who are less likely to file a claim pay less for their insurance than people who are more likely to file a claim.

Insurance scores predict the average claim behavior of a group of people with essentially the same credit history. People with low insurance scores tend to file more claims. Hence, based on the insurance scoring, the company may decide to accept a risk to be covered or not. If they decide to cover a risk even with a "not so good" insurance score, they may then decide to "load" the premium, meaning that they charge higher than normal or average in cases of doubt.

However, there are laws and regulations to protect the consumer against unnecessarily high premiums, and we all need to know some of the regulating agencies that may be approached in case of undue loading or rejections to provide a cover. There is a law in every state that prohibits insurers from setting rates that unfairly discriminate against any individual. The underwriting and rating processes are geared specifically to differentiate good risks from bad risks. Since insurance is a business, insurers favor those applicants that are least likely to suffer a loss.

Essentially, the system works almost the same way as the way bankers use the underwriting process for agreeing to extend a loan or not. If on balance they agree to extend the loan and the risks are greater than normal, the interest rate is a little higher for the additional risk that the lender is taking, or he "loads" a premium on the interest rate.

CLUE reports: There are two major property-claim databases, Comprehensive Loss Underwriting Exchange (CLUE) and Automated Property Loss Underwriting System (A-PLUS). Most people refer to the reports generated by either system as CLUE reports.

CLUE reports are generated by a company called ChoicePoint, a data-management company, and some 600 home-owning insurers contribute claims data to it. The Insurance Services Office, an insurance industry organization, runs A-PLUS, to which about 1,250 companies contribute. Insurers that contribute loss data can withdraw information from the exchange.

Before the availability of such computerized databases, insurance providers searched local records and asked for claims information from the applicant for insurance and his or her current insurer. This was extremely time-consuming and often resulted in inaccurate information. With computerization, the reports are produced almost instantaneously, and the information is more reliable, saving both time and money.

CLUE reports and the consumer: Like credit scores, consumers can get a copy of their own CLUE report for a small fee from ChoicePoint. CLUE reports are playing an increasingly important role in real estate transactions. Many buyers now stipulate that a CLUE report on a new home must be included with the real estate contract, and some state legislatures are considering making this a requirement for any real estate transaction.

Hence, as in case of credit scores, it is important that you keep your insurance history as clean as possible to ensure that you always get insurance coverage at a reasonable cost.

Glossary and Definitions of Financial Terms in Simple Words

Amortization: Amortization is a means of paying out a predetermined sum (the principal) plus interest over a fixed period of time, so that the principal is completely eliminated by the end of the term. This would be easy if interest weren't involved, since one could simply divide the principal amount into a certain number of payments and be done with it. The calculation involved requires some special mathematics, which requires amortization schedules prepared for this purpose. This amortization ensures that each payment should be the same amount and that a payment consists of some amount for principal reduction along with the interest calculated on the principal balance (including the principal part of the current payment).

Conventional or traditional loans: These are the best borrowings from all different aspects. The banks that extend this have a criterion of qualification for such loans. If the borrower passes the necessary test, then generally this is the best kind of money at a reasonable rate for the borrowers.

"Criticized" or "observed upon" loans: Those loan files that get an adverse remark from the auditors or regulators are called observed-upon or criticized loans. It is considered bad for the bank staff to have the loan files criticized, and there may be some further consequences for the working of the bank in terms of regulatory requirements.

Debt-to-equity ratio: This represents the relation between dollars you've borrowed and dollars you've invested in your business. This mathematical formula tells the lender how comfortable he should feel. For instance, if your debt is 80 and your equity is 20 (total investment being 100), the ratio is 4. This is usually the biggest number for the lender to accept to finance the project. The smaller this number, the more comfortable is lender, and vice versa. The more money the owners invest in their business, the easier it is to attract financing. Hence, if owners invest 40 and ask for 60 as debt (total investment being 100), it is more attractive to lender, since the ratio is only 1.5.

Factoring: See chapter 3.

Lease financing: This is generally used to acquire equipment, machinery, or tools of the trade. Since there is an additional middleman between the seller of that machine and the user, who also has to make profit, the rate of such money for the borrower is more expensive.

Liability: All the sums that are payable in actual or contingent upon some occurrence are the liabilities. For accounting purposes, there may be current and long-term liabilities, which are then matched with current and long-term assets for arriving at some percentages and ratios. These indirectly refer to the health of the business.

Over-leveraged company: If the debt is larger than acceptable, it is called over-leveraged. Meaning, if the investment is 10 and the debt is 90 (total investment being 100), it is a higher leverage than 20 to 80.

Profits and losses: This is the bottom-line amount in a profit and loss statement. Profit is the positive amount left after deducting from the revenue all the expenses pertaining to the business. Loss will be the negative amount. The taxes may have to be paid from this as per the IRS schedule.

Revenue: This is the amount of money generated by the sale of goods or services. Usually the size of a company is referred to by the size of revenue per year.

Venture capital: This is an amount of money extended to a project by an adventurer. He is generally able to sustain the loss if the whole or major portion of the amount is lost in the project. However, the arrangement is such that, if the project turns into profit, the reward for the venture capital is much better than other traditional investments.

Annex: Banking in the U.S.

To be able to understand the banking system in the U.S., we shall have to look into the history of banking. Traditionally, it has been unit private banking started by respectable people with substantial equity. Until the early part of last century, with only some tentative supervision, these banks kept on doing any business, which made money for them. The Great Depression of 1930 changed this. The Depression resulted in vast unemployment lasting for a long time and also caused the failure of thousands of banks that were not able to fulfill their obligations.

Glass-Steagall Act: This Act was passed in two stages, one in 1932 and another in 1933. This has remained one of the pillars of banking law since its passage. It has caused to erect a wall between commercial banking and investment banking. In effect, the law prevents banks from doing business on Wall Street, and vice versa. It is actually the Bank Act of 1933, which contains the provision to prevent the banks from indulging in securities businesses.

By 1933 the U.S. was in one of the worst depressions of its history. A quarter of the formerly working population was unemployed. The nation's banking system was chaotic. Over 11,000 banks had failed or had to merge, reducing the number of banks by 40%, from 25,000 to 14,000.

The governors of several states and President Roosevelt closed the banks on March 4, 1933, and they reopened on March 14, 1933. This was the longest "bank holiday," or forced lockout of banks, in the U.S. This was the result of the Depression, which caused a lack of confidence in people about banks. The shrinking of economy evidenced by rising unemployment, caused the run on

The Act, however, has not changed the most important weakness of the American banking system: the unit banking within states and the prohibition of nationwide banking. This structure is considered the principal reason for the failure of so many U.S. banks, some 90% of which were unit banks with under $2 million in assets. In contrast, Canada, which had nationwide banking, suffered no bank failures.

The Act established new approaches to financial regulation, the institution of deposit insurance, and the legal separation of most aspects of commercial and investment banking, with only a few exceptions like government securities.

The official green light for banks to sell insurance came with the U.S. Supreme Court's 1996 ruling in favor of Florida's Barnett Bank. In finding for Barnett Bank, the court reversed the Banking Act of 1933 (the Glass-Steagall Act), limiting the amount of income commercial banks could receive from the securities markets to 10%.

Banks are federally regulated. The insurance industry has federal and state regulations. However, it must be clear in everyone's mind that just because they get an insurance policy from a bank doesn't mean that policy is protected by the Federal Deposit Insurance Company, as their bank accounts are.

Index

Glass-Steagall Act 19, 45, 185, 186
Gross margin 94, 95
Guaranty 38, 62

L

Lease financing 14, 184
Letter of credit 39
Liability 152, 184
Limited-liability entities xv, 153, 154, 155
Limited partnership 155, 164
Line of credit 12, 15
Living trust 177
Loan application 31, 32
Loan package 65, 72
Loan proposal 68, 91
Logo 159, 160, 161

N

Net margin 95

O

Office of Small Business (OSB) 58
Operating cash flow 131
Operating margin 95

P

Partnership 13, 70, 154, 155, 156, 177
Planning 4, 127, 128, 152, 174, 176
Prepayment penalty 64, 89
Promissory note 112

R

Real estate 43, 82
Receivables 77, 81, 118
Reconstruction Finance Corporation (RFC) 57
Retail banking 45
Royalties 160, 161

S

SBA guaranty 61, 62, 63, 64
SBA prequalification program 64
Security agreement 112, 113
Smaller War Plants Corporation (SWPC) 57
Small Business Administration (SBA) xiv, 57, 58
Small Business Investment Company (SBIC) 58
Small Defense Plants Administration (SDPA) 58
Subordination 114

T

Term loan 12
Title insurance 172
Trusteeship 108, 109

U

Underwriting 104, 181

V

Venture capital 184

W

Will 141, 174
Working capital 131

About the Author

Dr. Barkat Charania has been an entrepreneur for almost five decades, since the age of fifteen. His endeavors include selling items such as toffees; trading utensils, cloth, jewelry, oriental carpets, automobile tires, gasoline, raw materials, and metals; and operating a private hospital of two hundred beds. Dr. Charania is an orthopedic surgeon trained in the United Kingdom. He has also received a degree in law and has pursued graduate studies in history.

Dr. Charania served as an advisor to World Health Organization and UNICEF. He presently serves on the boards of various organizations involved in real estate investments, trading fuel products and electricity, healthcare delivery, and banking.

All these varied experiences led him to establish close connections with banking, financing, and networking relationships. The material in this handbook is a direct reflection of his personal experiences in these fields and of his colleagues in the accounting, law, banking, and insurance industries.

www.ingramcontent.com/pod-product-compliance
Lightning Source LLC
Chambersburg PA
CBHW032000170526
45157CB00002B/477